**BODY BAG**

**BY**

**ROLLINS**

NOTE: THIS BOOK IS A COMPILATION OF TWO THIRTEEN SIXTY ONE, END TO END AND POLIO FLESH.

## OTHER BOOKS BY ROLLINS

**20**
TWO THIRTEEN SIXTY ONE
END TO END
POLIO FLESH
HALLUCINATIONS OF GRANDEUR
YOU CANT RUN FROM GOD
PISSING IN THE GENE POOL
WORKS
1000 WAYS TO DIE
KNIFE STREET

ROLLINS
POST OFFICE BOX 2461
REDONDO BEACH, CA 90278 USA
INFORMATION LINE: (213) 661-6515

COPYRIGHT 1988 BY ROLLINS
FIRST PRINTING

WHEN THEY DO WORK YOU GET DESTROYED: FUGAZI, THEO VAN ROCK, RATMAN, PUBLIC ENEMY, JAMES BROWN, HUBERT SELBY, MITCH BURY OF ADAMS MASS, JOE COLE.


Published 1989 by CREATION PRESS
8 Westgate Street,
London, E8
01 986 7196


European contact: ACTION PRESS
c/o Play it again Sam
67 rue de Cureghem,
1000 Bruxelles
32 2 514 1300

**BODY BAG**

SOUTHBAY, ARE THERE ANY REAL PEOPLE HERE AT ALL? HAVE YOU EVER BEEN TO 7-11? NOTHING BUT CELLOPHANE AND YOUTHS HUMPING THE VIDEO GAMES. 25 CENT VIDEO YOUTH, WHAT CULTURE! THOSE MACHINES BREED KILLERS, I'M SURE OF IT. GO, GO VIDEO YOUTH, GO TO THE STREET, HERE'S A QUARTER KILL A QUEER, KILL A NIGGER, KILL A COMMIE, KILL! KILL! KILL! I CAN SEE THEM NOW, STORMING INTO WESTWOOD ARMED TO THE TEETH W/AUTOMATIC WEAPONS AND QUARTERS. EDDIE VAN HALEN & MICHAEL JACKSON AT THE CONTROLS DISTRIBUTING QUARTERS AND BARKING OUT COMMANDS! THIS IS A SICK WORLD WE LIVE IN THAT'S FOR GODDAMN, SURE, ONLY EARTH COULD COME UP W/PHILADELPHIA.

. . .

My father took me to see "The Godfather" when it first came out. The theatre was packed full of people. The movie was underway and the people were very quiet. Behind us there was a large black guy. The black guy pulled out a bag of potato chips and opened them up. The wax paper made a bit of noise and my father said "Hey shut up!" Real loud. I sank into my seat and remained there for the rest of the film. I think it would have been real cool if (a) the guy smiled and offered my dad some chips (that would have chilled his shit pretty good) or if (b) the guy slapped my dad upside his head.

My father took me to McDonald's one Saturday when I was very young. It was springtime. We pulled into the parking lot and got out. There were two hippies parked next to us, a boy and a girl. On the side of their car they had some American flag stickers stuck on upside-down. My dad started yelling at them, he called them "pinkos," "fags," "commies," "hippies." He told them to get haircuts and to take those stickers off their car. The girl got real upset and ripped her shirt open, her breasts fell out, right there in the McDonald's parking lot. I don't know why she ripped her shirt open to express her agitation, maybe that's how you did it back then. It might have been kind of neat if the girl kicked him in the nuts or something.

. . .

I'M IN MY APARTMENT. MY LEFT FOOT
NAILED TO THE FLOOR. I JUST GO IN
CIRCLES. A LITTLE BLOOD SEEPS OUT.
I'LL BE HERE TOMORROW
IF I CAN MAKE IT THRU TODAY.
A LITTLE BLOOD SEEPS OUT.
THE DAYS PASS
LIKE PASSING YOUR HANDS THRU BROKEN
GLASS.
A LITTLE BLOOD SEEPS OUT.
I FEEL SOME PAIN HERE AND THERE
I FEEL THE DAYS PASSING   ME.
I CHOKE ON THE EXHAUST.
A LITTLEBLOOD SEEPS OUT.
. . .

I WANT TO TAKE A WALK
A LONG WALK
INTO THE DESERT
INTO THE HEAT
I SEE MY NAME
CARVED IN THE RUINS
I SEE MY NUMBER
CARVED IN THE RUINS

I CAN FINALLY SEE MYSELF

MY REFLECTION IN SAND
REFLECTED IN LIGHT
REFLECTED IN HEAT
I RAISE MY HANDS TO THE SKY
IT IS TIME TO DIE
IT'S ALWAYS TIME
THERE'S ALWAYS TIME TO DIE
DIDN'T IT ALWAYS SEEM LIKE TIME?
DIDN'T IT?
THE SUN BRINGS THE BLOOD TO BOIL
I DROP TO THE GROUND.

. . .

HE WAS EVERYTHING YOU COULD WANT IN A CHILD KILLER. HE LIVED ALONE. HE SENT LETTERS TO HIS MOM EVERYDAY, TELLING HER EXACTLY WHAT HE HAD DONE AND WHAT HE WANTED TO DO. HE PUT THE LETTERS IN AN ENVELOPE AND ADDRESSED IT "MOM, HEAVEN." HE MASTURBATED IN THE DARK, HE PICKED CRAB LICE FROM HIS SCROTUM AND BURST THEM BETWEEN HIS FRONT TEETH. WELL, HE HAD DONE IT, FOUR TIMES TOTAL, THREE IN ONE SUMMER, ONE BOY THREE GIRLS. THE BOY HAD BEEN FIRST, A DESTITUTE WOMAN HAD FOUND

THE BODY IN A DUMPSTER WHILST SEARCHING FOR FOOD. THE BOY'S PENIS AND TESTICLES HAD BEEN REMOVED AS WELL AS THE TONGUE AND EYES. THE POLICE DETECTIVES NEVER FOUND THEM AND WHY WOULD THEY? THEY WERE AT HOME IN THE FREEZER. THE GIRLS WERE FOUND IN ASSORTED PLACES, AND MUTILATED IN VARIOUS WAYS. THERE WERE SIMILARITIES HOWEVER, THE EYES, TONGUE AND NIPPLES HAD BEEN REMOVED FROM ALL THREE, ONE, THE THIRTEEN YEAR OLD, HAD REALLY TURNED HEADS AT THE CITY MORGUE. HE HAD TAKEN AN EMPTY MALT LIQUOR BOTTLE AND INSERTED IT SO FAR INTO HER VAGINA THAT THE NECK WAS DEEPLY LODGED IN HER LIVER. THE CORONERS REASONED THAT THE ONLY WAY HE COULD HAVE POSSIBLY DONE IT WAS TO HAVE GRABBED THE GIRL BY THE ANKLES AND TO HAVE INSERTED IT WITH HIS FOOT. WHATEVER, THE SUMMER WAS YOUNG AND HE WAS GETTING RESTLESS AND LONELY AGAIN.

. . .

THE CHILD KILLER, CUTS 'EM UP, GRABS ALL THE HEADLINES, LEAVES A BLOODY FUCKING MESS, AND WHO GETS THE CLEAN UP JOB? THE JANITOR THAT'S WHO. WHILE YOU ARE OUT RAPING AND SLASHING AND KILLING AND MAIMING, YOU NEVER EVEN THINK TO CLEAN UP YOUR MESS, YOU REALLY BURN ME UP! YOU ARE AN INCONSIDERATE SLOB! SURE, I LIKE TO HAVE A GOOD TIME, I LIKE TO GET A LITTLE CRAZY, BUT I AM A RESPONSIBLE CITIZEN! THE CITY OF LOS ANGELES HAS PROVIDED NUMEROUS WASTE RECEPTACLES FOR YOUR CONVENIENCE, USE THEM! THANK YOU!

. . .

NUMBERS ARE PERFECT, INFALLIBLE AND EVERLASTING -- YOU ARE NOT, REMEMBER THAT. NUMBERS ARE ALWAYS RIGHT IN THE END, YOU MAY SEE AN INCORRECT FIGURE BUT THAT IS NOT THE FAULT OF THE NUMBER, THE FAULT LIES IN THE PERSON CALCULATING THE NUMBERS. HOW MANY TIMES WILL YOUR HEART BEAT DURING YOUR LIFETIME, OF COURSE YOU DON'T KNOW! BUT THERE IS A NUMBER THAT WILL

PROVIDE YOU WITH THIS SMALL BIT OF INFORMATION. NUMBERS ARE DEPENDABLE! THE SUN MAY EXPLODE, YOU MAY LOSE YOUR JOB, YOU MIGHT NOT BE ABLE TO "GET IT UP" EVER AGAIN, BUT AT THE END OF THE DAY 5 IS 5, GET IT? GOOD! NUMBERS DO NOT CUT IN LINE AT LUNCH TIME, NUMBERS DO NOT WRITE BAD CHECKS, NUMBERS SOUND COOL, LIKE WHEN A FUCKING PIG GETS A CALL ON HIS PIG RADIO TO GO ANSWER A 511, YOU CAN GO TO BUY COFFEE AT 7-11. NUMBERS MAKE GOOD NAMES, LIKE AT A PARTY OR SOIREE, I ALWAYS WEAR A STICKER THAT HAS A MARTINI GLASS AND THE WORDS: "HI MY NAME IS:" PRINTED ON IT, UNDERNEATH THE PRINTING I WRITE IN "2-13-61." SO I CAN SAY HI, MY NAME IS 2-13-61, WHAT'S YOURS? THEN YOU CAN SAY TO GIRLS OR GUYS, "HEY YOU'RE REALLY THE BEES-KNEES -- WHAT'S YOUR NUMBER?"

. . .

HE CAN TAKE YOU TO
THE DESERT, HE CAN TELL
THE TIME BY JUST SAYING

SO. HE CAN TAKE YOU HOME, IF THAT'S WHERE YOU WANT TO GO. HE TOLD ME THE WORLD WAS GONNA GET HIT WITH A COAT OF BLACK PAINT THAT WAS NEVER GONNA COME OFF. HE IS INSANITY, PURE. I THINK HE WANTS TO BURN THE WORLD DOWN. I ACKNOWLEDGE MY LIFE THRU HIS DEATHS. WITH THE PERPETUAL DELIRIUM OF AN INSANE DREAM I THINK I KNOW JUST WHAT HE MEANS. I AM AFRAID OF THE ANIMALS HE UNDERSTANDS. IN A DREAM HE TOUCHED WITH A BURNING HAND.

. . .

YOU CLIMB, AND CLIMB. HAND OVER HAND.

YOU REACH THE TOP.
YOU STAND ON THE SHAKY EDGE OF YOUR HEART.
YOU LOOK AT HER EYES.
YOU LOOK INTO HER EYES.
YOU HOLD YOUR BREATH AND JUMP.
YOU LEAP INTO HER ARMS.
HER ARMS ARE AT HER SIDES.
YOU FALL PAST HER WINDOW
YOU HIT THE GROUND.
YOU ARE SHATTERED.
ALL BROKEN UP,
LIKE SOMEONE TAKING A BOTTLE,
AND DROPPING IT ONTO THE GROUND.
ALL BUSTED UP.
SHARP JAGGED BROKEN PIECES
OF YOURSELF
LYING ON THE GROUND.
YOU PUT THE PIECES BACK TOGETHER AGAIN.
THEY NEVER GO BACK QUITE THE SAME.
THE OUTSIDE IS SEAMLESS, SMOOTH.
BUT INSIDE,
BROKEN GLASS MIND AND A SOUL
WITH LITTLE CRACKS IN THE SIDES
AND LOOSE SPLINTERS AT THE BOTTOM.

THEY STAY TO REMIND YOU.
AT TIMES THE SOUL GLASS SPLINTERS
WILL GIVE YOU A JAB TO REMIND YOU OF
YOUR LEAP.
AFTER A TIME, WHEN YOU START CLIMBING
AGAIN, YOU WILL FORGET
ABOUT THE SOUL GLASS SPLINTERS.
SHE CAN BREAK YOUR FALL,
OR LET YOU
FALL AND BREAK.
AND EVERY TIME YOU JUMP
YOU JUST KNOW SHE'S GOING TO CATCH
YOU.
. . .

A MAN DROVE HIMSELF
INSANE
HE WAS DRIVEN
INSANE
AT LEAST HE
WAS DRIVEN
I DON'T KNOW
ABOUT YOU, BUT IT
SURE SEEMS
BETTER THAN JUST
SITTING AROUND

**TALKING ABOUT IT.**

. . .

**I WANT YOU TO
ACT LIKE A HUMAN
BEING, FOR YOU
IT IS AN ACT
MAKE THE MOVE
MAKE YOUR FLESH MOVE
GET UP
TELL ME WHAT
YOU'RE LOOKING AT
GET UP!
MAKE IT MOVE
MAKE YOUR FLESH MOVE
MAKE IT CRAWL
MAKE IT CRAWL
OH PLEASE,
DO SOMETHING.**

. . .

**SAY IF WE WERE IN A HOUSE THAT WAS BURNING DOWN AND THERE WAS TIME FOR ONLY ONE TO ESCAPE, I WOULD PUSH YOU AHEAD OF ME SO YOU WOULD BE THE ONE TO REACH SAFETY. I WOULD DIE HAPPY**

KNOWING THAT YOU WERE OK. IF WE WERE ON A SINKING SHIP AND THERE WAS ONLY ONE LIFE PRESERVER, I WOULD WRAP IT AROUND YOU AND TELL YOU TO REACH SHORE WITH ALL SPEED. I WOULD DIE FOR YOU, YES I WOULD.

. . .

I SIT IN A DIFFERENT JAIL HOUSE. I WRAP MY FINGERS AROUND MY JAILCELL EYES AND BEAT MY TIN CUP AGAINST MY RIBS. SOMEONE LEFT THE GATE TO THE FIELDS OF HUMANITY OPEN. ONE NIGHT I CREPT IN, WITH A JAIL HOUSE MIND, WITH A THOUGHT, WITH A WISH, AND I SLAUGHTERED THE FIELDS, I BURNED THEM TO THE GROUND.

. . .

LOOK AT THE PEOPLE DANCING IN THE FIELDS.
HUMAN HARVEST.
I WATCH ALL OF THOSE IN ATTENDANCE.
THRU SCARECROW EYES THE FIELDS ARE ON FIRE, AND EVERYBODY'S BURNING. PILES OF LOVERS, STACKED IN TWISTED

HEAPS, DOUSED WITH GASOLINE AND SET TO BURN. PILES OF DEAD BODIES BURNING. I LISTEN TO THE OIL CRACKLE OF SMOLDERING HAIR AND FLESH. I'M STILL ALIVE. I AM TOO EMPTY TO BURN. WHEN I CLOSE MY EYES I CAN STILL HEAR THEIR SCREAMS. I REMEMBER THEIR LAST DANCE, BEFORE I LIT THE FIELDS AFLAME. IT WAS BEAUTIFUL.

. . .

TONIGHT'S SUMMER NIGHT IS A DEAD MAN WRAPPED IN A WET BLANKET. I FOUND HIM FLOATING FACE UP IN MY ROOM. I'M LOST IN THIS SWAMP, SINKING IN THE QUICKSAND OF MY LONELINESS. SITTING HERE, SWEATING, CURSING AND SINKIN' ALL THE WHILE. MY HEART MAKING A DULL-DRUM SOUND AND I'M THINKING THAT MY LIFE IS A WAITING GAME AND I'M SINKIN' ALL THE WHILE.

. . .

MY MIND AND I HAD A MEETING, AND WE CAME TO THE CONCLUSION THAT YOU ARE GOING TO LET US DOWN. WE ARE HERE

EVERY MINUTE OF THE DAY GETTING READY FOR THE LET DOWN. SO WHEN YOU PUSH ME AWAY, I'LL JUST SAY OK, BECAUSE WE CAME TO THAT CONCLUSION A WHILE AGO. LIKE I SAID, WE WERE READY FOR THE LET DOWN. IF YOU ARE EVER WALKING DOWN THE WAY AND YOU SEE ME ON THE SIDE OF THE ROAD LYING BROKEN AND SCATTERED, YOU JUST KEEP WALKING, RIGHT ON BY.
. . .

I KNOW I'M HEAVY COMPANY TONIGHT. I'M SORRY. I HAVE NOTHING TRASHY OR VIOLENT TO READ TO YOU TONIGHT, SORRY, FRESH OUT. NOTHING ABOUT GIRLS GETTING FUCKED IN THE ASS WITH BUDWEISER BOTTLES, NOT A THING ABOUT GETTING FUCKED BY SOMEONE, OR GETTING FUCKED OVER BY SOMEONE. I KNOW THIS IS A TOUGH CROWD, I KNOW YOU ARE USED TO THE REAL NASTY STUFF BUT YOU'LL HAVE TO BEAR WITH ME, BECAUSE LIKE I SAID BEFORE, I'M FRESH OUT OF THAT STUFF. NO PASSAGES ON THE SUBJECTS OF RAPE, CUNTS, COCKS, VIOLENT SEX AND ALL THAT JAZZ, LIKE I SAID, FRESH OUT,

AND I KNOW THAT YOU HAVE YOUR STANDARDS OF FILTH AND DEGRADATION, I KNOW I'M NOT GOING TO MEASURE UP, I'M SORRY. I DID HAVE A TRASH BAG FULL OF STUFF ABOUT BIG BLACK GUYS EATING TENDER WHITE PUSSY AND THEN PARTYING DOWN WITH A BLOW TORCH. A THING ABOUT THE CUNT THAT FUCKED THE WORLD AND THEN DIED, A GIRL THAT GAVE SO MUCH HEAD THAT SHE SWEATED CUM -- AND THEN DIED. A PIECE CALLED "GUTTER TO HEAVEN" WHERE EVERYONE FUCKS AND THEN KILLS EACH OTHER OR KILLS THEMSELVES AND THEN A BIG RIVER OF URINE COMES A 'RIPPIN' DOWN THE WAY AND CARRIES THEM DOWN TO MACY'S OR SOME SHIT, HEY, I KNOW THIS IS GOING TO FALL SHORT BUT LIKE I SAID, SORRY, I'M FRESH OUT.

. . .

I DON'T THINK THAT THIS ROAD WILL EVER END. SOMETIMES I GET SO TIRED THAT I THINK I WILL FALL OFF. I HAVE LOOKED HIGH AND LOW AND I CAN'T FIND ANYONE ELSE HERE. THE NIGHTS ARE SO COLD

THAT I CAN'T SEEM TO EVER WARM UP. I HAVE BEEN OUT HERE FOR AWHILE AND I WILL PROBABLY BE OUT HERE FOREVER. I CAN TELL, THIS ROAD HATES ME, THIS ROAD DOES NOT WANT ME HERE. I DON'T KNOW WHERE ELSE TO GO. SOMETIMES I GET SO LONELY THAT I THINK I'M GONNA BREAK IN PIECES, LIKE BROKEN GLASS, LIKE A BOTTLE DROPPED ONTO PAVEMENT, ALL BROKE UP.

. . .

THERE WAS A CAR CRASH, A POWERFUL CAR CRASH. HEAPS OF TWISTED MUSCLE MACHINE. THE ENGINE DIED SCREAMING, WRAPPED ITS TEETH AROUND A TREE. IN THE BOWELS OF THE WRECK WAS A GIRL. THE MOST BEAUTIFUL GIRL I HAD EVER SEEN. THE CRASH HAD BEEN ABRUPT, CRUDE. BUT EVEN THIS COULD NOT MAR HER. BROKEN GLASS MADE A GLITTERING NECKLACE AROUND HER NECK. HER HEAD WAS CRUDELY THROWN BACK, SPLAYING BEAUTIFUL CHESTNUT BROWN HAIR AROUND HER SHOULDERS AND FACE. HER EYES WERE WIDE OPEN AND STARING OUT. IT'S

HARD FOR ME TO EXPLAIN WHAT HER EYES WERE SAYING, THEY HAD A LOOK OF WISE INNOCENCE, OF JADED VIRGINITY, I'LL NEVER FORGET HER EYES. HER FACE WAS COMPOSED, BEAUTIFUL, SAINT-LIKE. HER LEGS WERE RUDELY SPREAD AND BROKEN AS IF THE CAR HAD RAPED HER BEFORE I HAD GOTTEN THERE. ONE HAND RESTED ON HER THIGH AS IF TO PROTECT HERSELF FROM ATTACK AND THE OTHER WAS THROWN BACK OVER THE HEADREST WITH SUBMISSIVE ABANDON. THE NIGHT AIR WAS FULL OF HER PERFUME.

I NEVER SAW HER ALIVE, SHE NEVER LIED TO ME ONCE.

. . .

I SEE WALKING BOMBS ON THE STREET
HEARTS NOT BEATING, BUT TICKING
I AM TALKING ABOUT DETONATION!
YOU'RE IN McDONALD'S
AND SOME GUY'S HEAD EXPLODES.
BRAINS EVERYWHERE.
I THINK THERE IS SOME FAULTY CIRCUITRY HERE

YOU SEE SOME GUY IN A BUSINESS SUIT,
WALKING HOME FROM WORK,
LOOK AT HIM CLOSELY
HE'S SLUMPED OVER
THERE'S A LITTLE SMOKE COMING OUT OF ONE EAR
THERE IS A BUZZING, CRACKLING SOUND COMING FROM HIS HEAD
BLOWN FUSES
POOR MACHINE!
BUT IT'S OK
THE PARTS ARE INTERCHANGEABLE
WE'LL INSTALL A NEW ONE
. . .
I AM ALONE
EVERY MINUTE I THINK ABOUT MY GIRL
I BURIED HER UNDER THE FRONT PORCH
AND IN THE BACK YARD
MY FLEAS LEFT ME LAST NIGHT
MY LICE TOO
THEY USED TO PLAY SO MERRILY IN MY HAIR
I'LL MISS THEM
THE LEAVES IN THE TREE IN THE FRONT YARD
ARE DYING!

THEY DROP AND DIE
THEY CURL UP AND DIE
SOMETIMES I WISH I SHOULD CURL UP AND DIE
ONE OF THESE DAYS I WILL
I'LL WAKE UP AND I'LL BE DEAD
I'LL GET UP
AND GO ON DOWN
TO THE STORE
. . .

I AM MADE OF LEATHER
I AM COVERED WITH RUN & HYDE
I COME SO CHEAP
SO CHEAP
I COME UNDONE
I COME FROM WITHIN
I GOT NO HEART SO I CAN'T DIE
I GOT NO MIND SO I CAN'T LIE
COME ON!
UNTIE ME UP
. . .

THE GIRL WHO MOVES WITH RUSTLING MUSIC
SNAKES

SHE HAS A HEAD FULL OF SNAKES!
WHEN I SEE HER
I FEEL LIKE ONE OF THOSE SNAKES
WRITHING
SQUIRMING
DID YOU HEAR ME?
MEDUSA
MEDUSA
I BURN FOR YOU
SWEAT
MUSCLES PULL
MY HEART
WRITHING, SQUIRMING
LOVE ME ONCE
THEN TURN ME TO STONE
MEDUSA
SNAKES
MEDUSA
MEDUSA.
WHEN WILL THIS END.

. . .

YOU WANT TO TAKE ME
DOWN WITH YOU
I SEE YOUR EYES
I KNOW WHAT'S ON YOUR MIND

I'M NOT LIKE YOU
AND YOU HATE ME FOR IT
I'M NOT A DROWNING MAN
I GOT A MIND OF MY OWN
AND I'M GOING TO KEEP IT
I'M SORRY I CAN'T LET YOU
TAKE ME, DEFINE ME, STOP ME
I KNOW
YOU'LL TURN ON ME
BECAUSE I'M NOT LIKE YOU
. . .

IN A STATE OF DELIRIUM I DREAMT THAT I CAME UPON A FEMALE COCKROACH THE SIZE OF A GIRL. SHE SMILED AT ME AND TOLD ME TO COME CLOSER. SHE KISSED ME. THE FEELING OF HER BELLY SCALES AGAINST MY FLESH MADE ME CONVULSE AND SWEAT. WE MADE LOVE. SHE WRAPPED HER SIX LEGS AROUND MY BACK AND PULLED ME CLOSE. HER ANTENNAS LASHED MY BACK. NO GIRL EVER MADE ME FEEL LIKE THAT BEFORE, EVER. BY MORNING I WAS COVERED WITH SWEAT, BLOOD AND A NOISOME YELLOW-GREEN MUCUS. SHE HAD MY CHILDREN (TWENTY

OF THEM). THEY WERE SEMI-HUMAN IN FORM, COULD REPRODUCE IN WEEKS NOT YEARS AND COULD LIFT UP TO SIX TIMES THEIR OWN WEIGHT. WE ARE BREEDING, IN THE ALLEYS IN THE SEWERS IN THE BACK ROOMS AND BROTHELS. NOT A DAY GOES BY WHERE MY CHILDREN DON'T GROW IN SIZE & STRENGTH. WE ARE EVERYWHERE. YOU TRY TO KILL US WITH MOTELS AND POISON, THIS IS SNACK-FOOD FOR US. YOU WILL NEVER RID THE WORLD OF US, WE WILL RID THE WORLD OF YOU. YOU WILL WITNESS THE DESTRUCTION OF YOUR WORLD. YOU ARE GOING TO FALL.

. . .

I WOKE UP THIS MORNING IN THE TRUCK. I LIKE SLEEPING IN THE TRUCK. IT'S QUIET AND DARK. RAIN WAS FALLING ON THE ROOF. SOUNDED NICE. OUTSIDE I HEARD TIRES SCREECHING FOLLOWED BY A LOUD CRASH. I LOOKED OUT THE WINDOW. HEAD ON COLLISION. THE SONG "DEAD JOE," BY THE BIRTHDAY PARTY IMMEDIATELY CAME TO MIND. THERE WAS A CHILD LYING SPRAWLED ON THE SIDEWALK IN THE RAIN.

THE MOTHER WAS IN HYSTERICS. THE CHILD KEPT SCREAMING "MOMMY! MOMMY!" I TRIED TO IMAGINE WHAT THE MOTHER SAW WHEN SHE LOOKED DOWN AT HER CHILD. WAS THE CHILD'S HEAD BASHED IN, WHERE ANY BONES EXPOSED? WAS THE CHILD'S BLOOD MIXING WITH THE FALLING RAIN AND MAKING RIVULETS OF BLOODY WATER INTO THE GRASS? DID THEIR EYES MEET? WHEN THE CHILD WOULD SCREAM, THE MOTHER WOULD JERK AS IF HIT BY LIGHTNING. DO THE JERK MOM, C'MON MOM, DO IT IN THE RAIN, C'MON MA, JERK IT. USE YOUR HIPS MOM, JERK IT.

. . .

I PUT MY COCK IN A NOOSE
THE BARE BULB HANGING FROM THE
CEILING IS LIKE SOME KIND OF CANCEROUS
GROWTH, JUST HANGING AROUND.

LOVE AND HATE EXIST
ON BOTH SIDES OF A
ONE-SIDED COIN

I ENTER THE WOMB OF A SILENT, SULLEN

DEPRESSION, I WAIT TO BE HATCHED OUT.
I AM ALWAYS STILLBORN. COLD, BLUE,
BAD AS GOOD AS DEAD AS GONE AS NEVER
WAS IN THE FIRST PLACE.
THE LAST PLACE IS THE SAME AS THE
FIRST PLACE, ONLY NOW I'M MORE SKILLED
IN SELF-ABUSE. I TAKE LESSONS FROM THE
QUIET PHONE, THE UN-KNOCKED ON THE
DOOR, THE
UNOPENED MAILBOX AND THE CLOCK THAT WON'T
SHUT OFF. SOMEDAY, I'LL SUBSTITUTE A BULLET
FOR TWO TYLENOL.

SHE LIT MY SOUL AND INHALED DEEPLY
...FLICKING MY ASHES OCCASIONALLY.
FINALLY, SHE GROUND ME OUT.
AFTER A TIME, SHE REACHED FOR ANOTHER.
CRACKED
CRUMBLING
RUPTURED SOUL
SHATTERED
I WROTE OUT A ROAD MAP TO GET BACK
HOME

I THREW IT AWAY
HERE I AM
IN UNCERTAIN TIME
AND A SHAKY PLACE
AND THIS IS ALRIGHT
NOT SOMEHOW
BUT ALRIGHT
THIS ISN'T THE WAY IT IS
IT'S THE WAY IT IS AROUND THESE PARTS
. . .

HEY GIRL, HOW DOES IT FEEL WHEN HE COMES TO YOU ALL SWEATY AND GLASSY-EYED? HOW DOES IT FEEL WHEN HE GRABS A HANDFUL OF YOUR HAIR AND DRAGS YOU DOWN. HOW DOES IT FEEL WHEN YOU DON'T WANT TO AND HE CRACKS YOU UPSIDE YOUR HEAD? HOW DOES IT FEEL WHEN HE SAYS "I'M SORRY BABY, C'MON, DON'T CRY" AND HE STILL HAS NOT STOPPED WITH HIS HANDS, PULLING YOUR PANTIES DOWN TO YOUR KNEES WHILE HE LOOK YOU STRAIGHT IN THE EYE? TELL ME, HOW DOES THAT FEEL? HOW DOES IT FEEL WHEN HE HAS IT IN HIS HAND. HOW DOES IT FEEL WHEN HE'S ATTEMPTING TO PUT IT

IN YOU? NAVIGATING WITH HIS INDEX FINGER, LOOKING OVER HIS LEFT SHOULDER, TRYING TO ACT REAL SLICK? HOW DOES IT FEEL WHEN HE PUTS IT IN YOU? DOES YOUR FACE STILL HURT FROM WHERE HE SMACKED YOU? DO YOU HAVE SEX WITH TEARS IN YOUR EYES OFTEN? HOW DOES IT FEEL WHEN HE'S PUMPING AWAY, AND NOT EVEN LOOKING AT YOU. HOW DOES IT FEEL TO HAVE A PRICK MAKE YOU FEEL NONEXISTENT? TELL ME, HOW DOES THAT FEEL?

. . .

I AM THE END
I AM THE END
THE END OF EVERYTHING
ASHES, ASHES
I AM THE END
I AM THE LIVING END
I AM
THE END
I AM THE END OF ALL
AND IT ALL FALLS
IT ALL FALLS
IT ALL FALLS DOWN

I AM WHAT I AM
I AM THE END
. . .

I WISH I KISSED THAT GIRL IN THE SUMMERTIME, I WISHED I TOUCHED THAT GIRL IN THE SUMMERTIME. BUT I DIDN'T. HER SUMMER DRESSES WERE FLOWER PRINTS. I WANTED TO TOUCH THEM WITH MY HANDS. SHE CRIED IN FRONT OF ME, BUT NEVER OVER ME. AFTER ALL CONFESSIONS SUBMITTED, NO CRIMES COMMITTED, MY FEELINGS WERE OMITTED WITH A DROP OF THE EYES AND THE SLAM OF THE DOOR. SHE LEFT AN EMPTY HOUSE IN MY HEART. THE LIGHTS DON'T WORK ANYMORE, THE HEATER'S BROKEN. THE ROOF LEAKS, THE RENT IS OVERDUE, THE WALLS AND DOORS ARE ALL SMASHED OUT. I'M TRYING TO FIX IT UP YOU KNOW? BUT SO FAR, CONSTRUCTION'S MOVING MIGHTY SLOW.
. . .

IT'S RAINY TONIGHT. THE RAIN AND THE SMELL OF THE STREETS REMIND ME OF

WASHINGTON D.C. LIKE WALKING HOME FROM HAAGEN-DAZS TO MY APARTMENT THOSE WALKS DID ME GOOD. CLEARED MY HEAD OF A DAY'S WORTH OF SHIT AT WORK. THE RAIN MAKES ME REMEMBER WALKING FROM SIMON'S HOUSE W/CFE TO THE WISCONSIN AVENUE 7-11 TO GET SOME GINGER BEER. AND HOW ON THE SAME NIGHT I WALKED AND WROTE "WOUND UP." THAT WAS ABOUT 2 WEEKS SHY OF A YEAR AGO. I WOULD LIKE TO GO TO DC AGAIN FOR A VISIT, WOULD I? I DON'T KNOW. I LIKE IT THERE IN THE SUMMER, THE NIGHTS ESPECIALLY. I LIKE GEORGETOWN, NOT THE PLACES YOU WOULD THINK, BUT MY PLACES (MY BOOK, MY PEN, MY PLACES) LIKE MONTROSE PARK, Q STREET, P STREET, N STREET, R STREET, MY 7-11'S.

ALWAYS WALKING. "DID YOU SEE WHAT THEY DID? WHAT THEY DID?" TO THE PET SHOP, THEY TURNED MY PET SHOP INTO AN ITALIAN RESTAURANT. STEVE SOLD HAAGEN-DAZS TO SOME FOOL, THEY PUT VIDEO GAMES IN THE LITTLE TAVERN AND ACTUALLY KEEP THE PLACE CLEAN AND

DON'T LET BUMS SLEEP ON THE FLOOR BY THE CIGARETTE MACHINE. I CAN'T EVEN RECOGNIZE THE CALVERT DELI ANYMORE, NICKY'S PUB USES FROZEN PIZZAS, THEY JACK-HAMMERED THE OLD EUROPE'S PARKING LOT, THEY PUT BULLET-PROOF GLASS IN PEARSON'S LIQUOR STORE, DONALD THE DOG DIED AND SITS IN A HEAP OF ASHES IN A BROWN PLASTIC BOX IN THE HALLWAY, THE MACARTHUR THEATRE TURNED INTO THE MACARTHUR 1-2-3. I'M 23 AND I SOUND LIKE I'M 55.

. . .

MY GHETTO
MY GHETTO
MY GHETTO
MY GHETTO GETS GETTING AND IT PULLS YOU IN
SEE THAT MANGY BLACK DOG LOOKING AT YOU
THRU ONE GOOD EYE?
YOU KNOW THAT BEAST IS FROM MY GHETTO
BECAUSE HE IS HUNGRY, AND LOW RUNNING

YOUR GHETTO GETS GETTING AND IT INVITES YOU IN
YOU WALK INTO MY GHETTO AND I HAND YOU A
SACK OF SAD BAD TRASH
SLAP YOU ON THE BACK AND SAY: "HOWDY, GLAD
YOU COULD COME ON DOWN!"

MY GHETTO GETS IT RIGHT AND SUNSHINE IGNORES
THIS HEAP OF BAD TIMING

MY GHETTO GETS HORNY AND IT SUCKS YOU IN
DO YOU SEE THOSE BOSS HOT RODS SLITHER BY?
YOU KNOW THOSE HEAPS ARE FROM MY GHETTO,
BECAUSE THEY ARE WRECKED AND LOW RIDING.

MY GHETTO GETS DESPERATE AND IT DRAGS YOU
IN.

DIG MY TRASH!
DIG MY TRASH!
HEAR MY CRY OF LOVE OVER THE BUZZ OF ONE
THOUSAND FLIES!
STAY WITH ME!
STAY WITH ME!
FOR A MOMENT OR FOREVER.
BECAUSE I GOT NOTHING AND I'LL GIVE IT ALL TO
YOU.
. . .

DADDY, YOU ARE IN YOUR BED ASLEEP
YOUR WIFE IS LYING NEXT TO YOU
SHE IS YOURS YOUR WOMAN
SHE' YOURS
I HAVE COME TO YOUR HOUSE
IN YOUR SLEEP YOU FEEL A
SHARP PAIN IN YOUR HEAD
I HAVE JUST SLAPPED YOU.
YOU ARE AWAKE, YOUR EYES WIDEN
IN FEAR, IT'S DARK, YOU DON'T
RECOGNIZE ME, OUR EYES MEET, I'M
LOOKING IN YOU, THRU YOU MY EYES ARE
LIKE TWO BULLETS RIPPING THRU YOUR

FACE. THE TABLES HAVE TURNED, IT'S GOOD NOW, YOUR WIFE HAS TURNED INTO A MASS OF PUTRID BLACK TAR AND IS OOZING OFF THE BED. I HAVE MUSCLES, THEY ARE STRONG, I CAN UTILIZE CRUSHING POWER. YOU ARE OLDER, WEAK, YOUR BONES ARE BRITTLE, YOU ARE COMPLETELY DEFENSELESS, I KNOW THIS AND FULLY TAKE ADVANTAGE OF IT. YOUR MOUTH IS OPEN, YOUR JAW IS WORKING, YOU ARE MAKING FAINT RASPING SOUNDS, BUT NO WORDS COME FROM YOUR MOUTH. GET UP! GET UP! I TOLD YOU TO GET UP AND YOU DO. NOW, SAY MY NAME, TELL ME WHO I AM, YOU SAY NOTHING, YOU ARE MAKING SLIGHT CHOKING SOUNDS, WHAT'S MY NAME, WHO AM I? DO YOU REMEMBER ME? I AM 2-13-61, I AM 2-13-61. MY LEFT FIST COMES STRAIGHT AT YOU, YOU SEE IT IN SLOW MOTION, YOUR FACE EXPLODES LIKE A PANE OF GLASS, SOMETHING BROKE, YOUR RIGHT CHEEK BONE IS CRUSHING COMPLETELY. YOU WOULD FALL TO THE GROUND IF I DID NOT HAVE A HOLD OF YOUR TRACHEA, I'M NOT EVEN SWEATING, THIS IS EASY, YOU ARE OLD AND WEAK,

SIMILAR TO BEATING A CHILD. YOU
REMEMBER NOW. YOU ARE SEEING BRIGHT
BLUE FLASHES AND SPOTS IN YOUR EYES, I
AM SQUEEZING YOUR TRACHEA SHUT, THE
CARTILAGE MAKES A RUBBERY SNAP-
CRACK-POP AS I CRUSH IT. I NOW START
SHAKING YOU BY IT. YOUR FEET ARE OFF
THE GROUND THEY DANGLE AS I SHAKE YOU
HEY DAD
HEY DAD
I LEARNED
I LEARNED RESPECT
I LEARNED DISCIPLINE
I HAVE STRENGTH
YOUR EYES ARE RIVETED TO THE CEILING
YOU SEE 2-13-61
CLEARLY
PERFECTLY
LIKE A CHILD.
. . .

SOME OF US LIVE IN THE DARK. WE NEVER
SEE THE LIGHT. UNLESS IT COMES THRU
THE WINDOW. STREETLIGHT AT NIGHT.
CREEPS THRU THE VENETIAN BLINDS AND
LAYS BROKEN AND SCATTERED ON THE

FLOOR. SOME OF US WAIT IN THE DARK. QUIETLY. PATIENTLY. SHARPENING OUR CLAWS WAITING FOR YOU. TO. SLIP. JUST ONCE. OUR BODIES ARE WARM. OUR MUSCLES ARE TIGHT. WE PRESS OUR EYES UP TO THE KEY HOLE AND LOOK AROUND. WE WAIT IN THE DARK, GRINDING OUR TEETH. WAITING. WAITING FOR YOU TO SLIP JUST ONCE.

. . .

I LIVE IN DISGUISE
I MOVE FROM STATION TO STATION
MY DREAMS SMASH LIKE GLASS ACTS IN
JAGGED
FORMATION
LIKE THE FOOL THAT I AM I SWALLOW THE
SLIVERS
AND SPIT DEAD EMPTY SONGS IN THE FACE
OF MISS
GIVERS

MEMORIES GET PULLED LIKE TEETH FROM
THE SHELF
I LOOK IN THE MIRROR BUT CAN'T SEE
MYSELF

**THE ONE THAT I CAN'T SEE IS THE ONE THAT I AM**
**THE ONE THAT I CAN'T SEE IS THE ONE IN DEMAND**

**ALONE**
**DON'T YOU KNOW**
**ALONE**
**LIKE ALWAYS**
**YOU'RE ALONE**
**IN THE END**
**ALONE**
**NO MATTER WHAT YOU SAY**
**ALONE**
**BY YOURSELF EVERY DAY**
**YOU'RE ALONE**
**GIVE YOUR GRIEF TO SOMEONE ELSE**
**ALONE**
**IT'S SUCH A DESPERATE GRAB**
**YOU'RE ALONE**
**ONCE YOU GO, YOU KNOW**
**YOU'RE ALONE**
**. . .**

**I BEAT MY WOMAN**
**WITH MY HANDS**

**EVERY TIME SHE COMES AROUND
I STAND HER UP AND SLAP HER DOWN
DO I MAKE MYSELF PERFECTLY CLEAR?
GOOD
YOU SEE
SHE WON'T SHUT UP
THE SOUND OF HER VOICE DRIVES ME OUT
OF MY
MIND
YOU CAN UNDERSTAND THAT CAN'T YOU?
I THOUGHT SO
I KNEW YOU WOULD
COME HERE BABY
OK
STOP CRYING
BABY
SHUT UP
. . .**

**IN THE DARK UNMOVING STILL OF THE
NIGHT
TWO LOVERS
THEIR BODIES TWIST & COIL
LIKE LOOPS
ON A HANGMAN'S NOOSE
AS THE SUN APPROACHES**

THEY SHRINK AND SEPARATE
AND SPEAK IN HUMAN TONES
DEATH TRIP
IN HERE
RIGHT NOW
. . .


MY VISION OF YOU IS MARRED BY SIGHT
THE THINGS I FEEL ARE NULLIFIED BY SENSE
THE THINGS I WANT FROM YOU
THE THINGS I WANT TO DO TO YOU
THE THINGS I WANT TO DO TO MYSELF
HERE COMES THE DUST
. . .

I KNOW THIS GIRL NAMED LYDIA LUNCH. SHE IS FROM NEW YORK. SHE IS REAL NEAT IN MY OPINION, LYDIA LUNCH TURNED ME ON TO A LOT OF GOOD STUFF, SUCH AS: EINSTURZENDE NEUBAUTEN, THE SWANS, HENRY MILLER, CHARLES BUKOWSKI, SONIC YOUTH, MARCY, RANDY AND JESSAMY. LYDIA LUNCH HAS BALLS, LYDIA LUNCH IS PRETENTIOUS, LYDIA LUNCH DELIVERS, LYDIA LUNCH IS TOUGH ON THE OUTSIDE

AND PRETTY TOUGH ON THE INSIDE. I HAVE SEEN HER SMILE A FEW TIMES AND IT WAS VERY NICE. THIS GUY STABBED HER ONCE. I GAVE HER A BLACK EYE WHEN WE DID A FILM TOGETHER. MR. GINN CALLS HER LYDIA SUPPER AND SHE'S OK BY ME.

. . .

I WAS IN A MENS ROOM AT ONE OF THOSE BIG GAS-REST-FOOD STOPS. AT THE URINAL I SAW SIX MEN PULL DOWN THEIR ZIPPERS AND PULL OUT THEIR COCKS ALMOST SIMULTANEOUSLY, IT WAS FANTASTIC, LIKE A FIRING SQUAD, OR LIKE SOME KIND OF SECRET MASONIC PUD GRAB RITUAL. MEN ACT DIFFERENT IN THE MENS ROOM. THEY DON'T TALK MUCH, AND IF THEY DO IT'S REAL LOUD AS IF TO SAY "HEY I'M NOT AFRAID TO TALK IN THE MENS ROOM!" THEY ACT VERY MAN-LIKE IN THE MENS ROOM LEST SOMEONE THINK THEY ARE GAY, OR GIRLISH. THERE ARE NO WEAKLINGS IN THE MENS ROOM! WE ARE IN THE MENS ROOM WE HAVE OUR COCKS IN OUR HANDS WE ARE URINATING "OUR WAY" RIGHT. A MAN WHO IS HEN-PECKED AND OWNED BY HIS

**WIFE OR GIRLFRIEND, TRANSFORMS INTO A VIRTUAL BEDROCK OF MASCULINITY UPON ENTERING THE MENS ROOM. IT'S A TEMPORARY CLUB, WHERE MEN, UNITED BY A NEED TO URINATE, ARE MEN.**

**. . .**

**THE JUNKMAN SEES EVERYTHING
PICKING UP ODDS AND ENDS
AND DO YOU KNOW HOW?
BECAUSE HE'S SEEN HIS LIFE
WRITTEN IN THE FILTH
WRITTEN ON THE SHIT THAT HANGS ON WALLS
THE STUFF THAT STARES BACK AND TELLS YOU
WHAT
HE HEARD ABOUT HIMSELF AT SOME FUCKIN' PARTY.
NOW HIS LIFE IS BACKGROUND MUSIC
HE FOUND HIS LIFE IN A PILE OF TRASH,
OVER BY MADAM'S ORGAN, HE'S BEEN WEARING IT
EVER SINCE – THE JUNKMAN.
OTHER'S WASTE IS HIS LIFE.
THE JUNKMAN**

. . .

**THE SOUND I FEEL THE MOST IS THE STILL, NIGHT AIR, ONLY BROKEN BY THE SONG OF A BIRD SOMEWHERE UP IN A TREE. HAVE YOU EVER BEEN OUT THERE, SWALLOWED UP IN THAT INKY NIGHT AIR? THE SMELL OF THE TREES AND LAWNS AND STREETS, I FEEL THE BEST WHEN I'M THERE, ALONE, I AM ALWAYS ALONE THERE. MY MIND'S KNOTS CAN COME UNTIED, I CAN CLOSE MY EYES, LET OUT A BREATH AND MY LIFE AS I KNOW IT (A JOURNEY OF TORMENT) BECOMES MORE EXACTING, MY EYES DULL AND MY HEAD HANGS, DRUNK ON NIGHT AIR.**

. . .

**SATURDAY NIGHT ON "THE STRIP." I'M LOOKING FORWARD TO MY GRILLED CHEESE/FRENCH-FRIED POTATOES THING. SITTING IN DENNY'S CRYSTALLINE WINDOW WATCH. NIGHTCRAWLERS AND GLITTERED FLY BY FREAKS — FREAK OUT EVERYTHING WITH THEIR SIDEWALK PARADE. IT'S SLEAZE-WALTZ AND I LIKE IT.**

. . .

I HATE TO WANT
YOU MAKE ME WANT
I HATE TO WANT
YOU MAKE ME WANT YOU
I HATE TO WANT
YOU MAKE ME WANT TO HURT YOU
I HATE TO WANT
IT HURTS TO WANT
I HATE TO WANT
I WANT TO WANT

    I SAW HER
    SHE WAS SURROUNDED BY LIGHT
    I PUT MY ARMS OUT
    I WANTED TO TOUCH HER
    I RAN TOWARD HER
    I PUT MY ARMS OUT
    I CAME TO HER
    SHE PUSHED ME AWAY
    I SMASHED HER FACE IN
    I WANTED HER TO WANT ME
    I WANTED HER TO WANT ME
    SHE DIDN'T WANT ME
    I SMASHED HER FACE IN

**SHE WAS:**
**PORCELAIN UNDER MY FIST**
**PORCELAIN CUT MY KNUCKLES**
**I WANTED HER TO WANT ME**

**THE LIGHT REFLECTS FROM HER HAIR / SHE CARRIES LIGHT IN HER HEART / SHE RADIATES / IF SHE TOUCHED ME I WOULD HEAL / SHE WALKS TOWARD ME / SHE WALKS RIGHT PAST ME / SHE WALKS AWAY.**
**. . .**

**I POURED SALT ON A LARGE SLUG. I WATCHED HOW THE SLUG WRITHED AND SQUIRMED. THE SLUG TRIED TO ESCAPE ME AND MY BURNING SALT. THE SLUG MADE NO SOUND. I AM SURE IF I WAS TURNED INSIDE-OUT AND DIPPED IN SALT, I WOULD SCREAM. I REMEMBER HOW THE SLUG GLISTENED AND RESPIRATED -- UNTIL I PUT THE SALT ON IT. I REMEMBER HOW IT TRIED TO GET AWAY, SECRETING YELLOW-GREEN MUCUS IN GREAT QUANTITIES THAT BUBBLED SLIGHTLY. MY FASCINATION TURNED INTO REVULSION AS THE SLUG WRITHED AND TOSSED FROM SIDE TO SIDE,**

SECRETING EVEN MORE YELLOW-GREEN MUCUS TO TRY AND BEAT THE SALT. IT WAS A LOSING BATTLE FOR THE SLUG, BECAUSE WHEN THE SLUG HAD SUCCEEDED IN RUBBING OFF SOME OF THE SALT, I WOULD SIMPLY TURN THE SALT SHAKER OVER ON THE SLUG AND THE GAME WOULD START AGAIN. EVENTUALLY I GOT BORED AND LEFT THE SLUG, STILL WRITHING, TRYING IN VAIN TO GET FREE OF THE SALT BATH THAT WOULD EVENTUALLY SUCK THE SLUG DRY.

–LATER I IMAGINED THAT MY WHOLE BODY WAS A TONGUE, AND I WAS DIPPED IN SALT.
. . .

HOME. THE STREETS LIE, THE SIDEWALKS LIE, YOU CAN TRY TO READ IT BUT YOU'RE GONNA GET IT WRONG. THE SUMMER EVENINGS BURN AND MELT AND THE NIGHTS GLITTER, BUT THEY LIE. UNDERNEATH THE STREETS THERE IS A RIVER THAT MOVES LIKE A SNAKE. IT MOVES WITH SMOOTH, UNDULATING, CRIPPLING MUSCLE POWER. IT CHOKES AND DROWNS AND TRIPS AND

**STRANGLES AND LURES AND SAYS "COME HERE, STAY WITH ME" AND IT LIES.**

**. . .**

**I SAW A MAN SLITHER DOWN FOUR BLOCKS OF GUTTER WITH HIS FACE PRESSED AGAINST THE GROUND, CALLED HIMSELF THE SNAKE MAN, SAID HE COULD DO JUST ABOUT ANYTHING, DIDN'T SAY A WORD ABOUT RIGHT OR WRONG OR ONCE OR TWICE, HE JUST TALKED ABOUT DOING IT. HE BLED DIRT, HE WAS DOWN IN THE GUTTER, CRAWLING LOW, HE WAS INVINCIBLE.**

**I SAW A MAN JAM A NEEDLE INTO HIS ARM, LOOKED MY WAY AND TOLD ME HE WAS FREE.**

**I SAW A MAN WHO HAD CRIED SO MUCH THAT HE HAD TRENCHES BORED INTO HIS FACE FROM THE RIVER OF TEARS. HE HAD HIS HEAD IN A VICE AND EVERY ONCE IN A WHILE HE WOULD GIVE IT A LITTLE TWIST.**

I SAW A MAN WHO WAS SO RUN DOWN THAT HE WAS PISSING BLUE, HE WAS PISSING THE BLUES, NOW THAT'S WHAT I CALL BLUE.

. . .

...TO THE ASTONISHMENT AND HORROR OF THE CROWD THAT ENCIRCLED HIM, THE CHICKEN MAN HAD REACHED DOWN HIS THROAT WITH HIS BARE HAND AND HAD PULLED OUT HIS HEART AND WAS NOW HOLDING IT IN THE FACES OF THE PEOPLE THAT HAD PAID 25 CENTS TO SEE HIM PERFORM. HEART IN HAND, HE STOOD, FEET PLANTED SOLIDLY. THE PEOPLE SAW THAT THIS WAS A HUMAN HEART, HIS HEART, NO CHICKEN HEART, THIS WAS A MAN, HUMAN BEING, NO FREAK. HE SCREAMED: "YOU ARE A BUNCH OF FREAKS!" — ALL EYES DROPPED TO THE GROUND. THE CHICKEN MAN ROLLED HIS EYES, GRINNED SLIGHTLY AND SHOVED HIS HEART BACK DOWN HIS THROAT, THE SHOW WAS OVER.

. . .

What is it? Is it my hair? Am I ugly? I know, I'm boring, that's what it is, I'm a drag to be around. I don't understand, maybe I don't hammer down hard enough, I'm spineless, that's it, please make me understand because all the shit hurts — a lot. Frustration, all locked up. I am stupid. For the rest of the day I will try not to be so stupid. I'll try to keep the parts together. No! I don't ask for much, I should ask for a lot, then maybe I might get some. Everyone seems to have it together a lot more than I. I know I'm fucked up in the head, but Johnson, open the gates, it's getting stuffy in here! Holy cats! I learn over and over. Slowly, over time, the pain goes away. And you say: "I won't play that game again, hey man! I don't play that game!" Well that's just another game to play. With all this playing going on, how does any work ever get done?/She: Is a beautiful girl, her neck alone is worth at least three pages of fine print. She: Is a smart girl, she, is, smart, yes, smart. She: Is nice, it feels good to be around her. When I am with her I feel great. She: Is a popular girl, she knows a lot of people and a lot of people know her. She: Is busy, she is always doing something, now when I told you she was popular, I wasn't kidding, hey! You should see this girl, her eyes warm you right up. This girl is special, when I see her I smile. You should see her smile, I don't know about you, but when she smiles at me, I want to grab her. You should see this girl, she is always happy about something. A bit earlier, I told you that she is beautiful, well she is! You would not forget her once you saw her and she...lives far away/Rollins out.

. . .

I HAD THIS DREAM LAST NIGHT WHILE I WAS SLEEPING IN THE TRUCK. I DON'T KNOW WHAT IT MEANS BUT HERE IS WHAT HAPPENED: I SAW A VAN GOING DOWN A ROAD THAT TRAILED DOWN A MOUNTAIN. CHARLES MANSON AND SOME GIRLS WERE IN IT. I WAS WATCHING THE WHOLE THING FROM ABOVE. MANSON WAS DRIVING REAL FAST, I KNEW THAT THEY WERE GOING TO CRASH. THE VAN TOOK A SHARP TURN, MUCH TOO FAST. THE VAN FLEW OFF THE SIDE OF THE MOUNTAIN AND WENT SAILING THRU THE AIR. THE VAN SMASHED DOWN

ON FLAT GROUND, BOUNCED UP IN THE AIR AND DISAPPEARED. THEN I SAW MANSON, HE WAS LYING IN THE SNOW, DEAD. HIS BODY WAS STRETCHED OUT IN THE SHAPE OF A CROSS. HIS FACE WAS TWISTED AND SCARRED FROM WHEN HE WAS TORCHED IN HIS CELL. EVEN THOUGH THE SCARRING WAS MASSIVE, I COULD SEE THAT HE LOOKED VERY YOUNG. HIS EYES WERE OPEN AND HAD A LOOK OF PIERCING AWARENESS. I COULD SEE THE SWASTIKA CARVED INTO HIS FOREHEAD. RIGHT ABOVE THE SWASTIKA WAS AN "X" FRESHLY CARVED AND BLEEDING FREELY. I WOKE UP AND COULD NOT GET BACK TO SLEEP.

. . .

DON'T SHOW ME TO THE DOOR
JUST SHOW ME TO THE FLOOR
AND I'LL CRAWL ON HOME
OH PLEASE MISS, DON'T MISUNDERSTAND ME
I JUST WANT TO FUCK YOU
I DON'T WANT TO FUCK WITH YOU
I JUST WANT TO FUCK YOU
SO SING MY SONG AND BEAT MY GONG

I'M DEAD AND GONE BUT NOT DEAD YET!
I'M SORRY FOR NOT BEING SORRY THAT I'M NOT
SORRY.
DON'T SHOW ME TO THE DOOR, JUST SHOW ME TO THE FLOOR AND I'LL MAKE LIKE A SNAKE AND CRAWL FOR REAL. NO USELESS LIMBS FLAILING AROUND, I'M SO LOW THAT I FLIRT WITH THE DUST, I FLIRT WITH THE DIRT SO HAWZA BOUTA DATE, HOWZA BOUTA
NIGHT ON ME ON YOU ON THE FLOOR?
—AND WE CAN CRAWL FOR REAL
CAN YOU GET LOWER THAN LOW-LIFE?

. . .

SOMETHING INSIDE
SOMETHING FROM UNDERNEATH
FLOWER
DEAD
GIRL
STREET
SOMETHING GROWING
SOMETHING IS GOING ON
HIT
CRY

**GIRL**
**RAIN**
**NOT AGAIN**
**PLAY IT AGAIN**
**FADE**
**EYES**
**GIRL**
**HOUSE**
**ROOM**
**GREY**
**DIRT**
**WASTE**
. . .

I REMEMBER I SAID TO IAN, SOMETHING ALONG THE LINES OF: "WE HAD THE BEST GOOD TIMES ANYONE EVER HAD." HE AND I BOTH AGREED THAT WHILE THERE ARE SOME REALLY GREAT DAYS, SOME REAL GOOD TIMES, THEY REALLY DON'T SEEM TO ROLL LIKE THEY USED TO. I KNOW THAT SOUNDS STUPID, LIKE LET THE GOOD TIMES ROLL, BUT THEY USED TO SEEM ENDLESS. YOU WOULD LOOK OVER THE HOOD OF YOUR CAR INTO THE STREET AND IT WAS GOOD. TIME GOES BY AND I BECOME LESS

BLIND OR I CAN LOOK BACK AND SEE MORE OR SOMETHING, DO YOU KNOW WHAT I MEAN?

I GET TIRED OF THE SUMMER TIME. THE PEOPLE WITH THEIR DATES, GETTING DRUNK, LAUGHING, HAVING A GOOD TIME, FUCKING WITH ME. I'M SO BUSY HAVING THE TIME OF MY LIFE THAT SOMETIMES I JUST WANT TO CURL UP AND DIE, BUT THAT'S ONLY SOMETIMES, LIKE SOMETIMES WHEN YOU'RE AT A PARTY OR YOU'RE HANGING OUT AND YOU'RE WITH ALL THESE PEOPLE AND YOU FEEL MORE ALONE THAN IF YOU WERE LOST IN THE DESERT. YOU FEEL LONELY-BLUE-FIT-TO-DIE, AND THE MORE PEOPLE AROUND YOU, THE MORE ALONE YOU SEEM TO BE? WELL, WHAT IF YOU WERE ON A STAGE WITH ALL THESE LIGHTS ON YOU, WITH ALL THESE PEOPLE LOOKING AT YOU, COMING TO SEE YOU, CALLING OUT YOUR NAME, MIGHT MAKE YOU FEEL KIND OF FUNNY, NOT LIKE FUNNY HA HA FUNNY, BUT FUNNY LIKE YOU COME FROM A DIFFERENT PLANET? AND YOU KNOW THAT YOU COULD QUIT ANYTIME YOU

WANT. YOU MIGHT THINK, WHY CAN'T I HAVE ONE WITHOUT THE OTHER, OR NEITHER, OR BOTH, BUT NOT FEEL IT SO HARD, OR SOMETHING, GOOD TIMES, GOOD TIMES.

. . .

SHE WAS MADE OF GLASS, SHE BROKE IN MY ARMS. THE SHARDS CUT SO CLEAN, SO DEEP, SO GOOD. MY HEART BLED THE ONLY SONG IT KNEW. IT HURT TO PULL OUT THE SLIVERS BUT I KNEW THAT I COULDN'T BLEED ANYMORE, I HAD LOST TOO MUCH BLOOD ALREADY. NOW I REMAIN, SCARRED AND REGAINING STRENGTH.

. . .

THE RITUAL
THE RITUAL
THE RITUAL, SAYING THANK-YOU
WHEN I MEAN FUCK-YOU.
THE RITUAL HAS BEEN BEATEN INTO MY SKULL
THE RITUAL
THE RITUAL CALLED MY NUMBER
AND THEY PUT ME UP HERE

AND KILLED ME WITH STONES.
I'VE GOT THE RITUAL BORED INTO MY SKIN,
I'VE GOT THE
RITUAL TATTOOED INTO MY BRAIN
THE RITUAL
THE RITUAL
THE RITUAL TURNED ON ME
LIKE A CORNERED ANIMAL,
I WAS SO CLOSE I COULD SEE ITS TEETH.
THE RITUAL WON'T LET ME SLEEP
I LAY AWAKE IN BED
WITH MY BRAIN SCREAMING:
2-13-61 — 2-13-61 — 2-13-61
THE RITUAL WON'T LET ME SAY "I LOVE YOU"
THE RITUAL WON'T LET ME
I BLEED FOR THE RITUAL
THE RITUAL TURNS ME ON
THE RITUAL TURNS ON ME
THE RITUAL HANGS ABOVE ME
LIKE A DEAD MAN SWINGIN'
THE RITUAL
THE RITUAL
SEE THE SCARS, REMEMBER THE BEATINGS?
REMEMBER,
REMEMBER THE RITUAL?
THE NIGHT GIVES BIRTH

**TO UGLY DEPRESSION—CHILDREN
WHO TUG AT YOU AND SCREAM:
MOMMY-DADDY! MOMMY-DADDY!
THE STRANGER YOU RECOGNIZE, SELF-
INFLICTION
ALONE IN YOUR ROOM WITH SELF ABUSE.
A VICE ON YOUR BRAIN.
YOUR HANDS KNOW
HOW TO CUT AND FIX AND STICK
WHATEVER-WHEREVER
HEAR IT POUNDING IN YOUR EARS
IT'S THE RITUAL
YOUR FISTS-YOUR TEARS-THE BLOOD
THE STRENGTH TO FEEL IT OVER AND OVER
IT'S THE RITUAL
. . .**

**THIS GUY CAME HOME FROM HIS JOB. HE WAS A COMPUTER DATA-RESEARCH-STATISTICS ANALYST OR SOME SHIT, I DON'T KNOW FOR SURE, BUT LIKE I SAID, THE GUY CAME HOME. HOME WAS THIS APARTMENT WITH THE FRONT DOORS FACING THE STREET, AND THE BACK DOORS GOING INTO THE BACKYARD COMMUNAL LEISURE AREA. HE HAD A WIFE AND A LITTLE GIRL, I THINK**

HER NAME WAS HEATHER OR FAWN OR SOMETHING THAT SOUNDED LIKE A NAME FROM THE BRADY BUNCH. THE GUY GETS OUT OF HIS CAR, AND HE SMELLS SOMETHING COOKING IN THE LEISURE AREA. WELL, HE GOES AROUND THE BACK WAY, YOU KNOW, SURPRISE THE WIFE (MAYBE GET A LITTLE AFTER THE NEWS). THERE'S SOMETHING COOKING ALRIGHT, THERE IS A HUMAN LEG SIZZLING ON THE PATIO GRILL, CUT OFF RIGHT BELOW THE BUTTOCK, WITH THE FOOT STILL INTACT. HE WAS OVERCOME WITH SHOCK, FOLLOWED IMMEDIATELY BY AN IMMENSE WAVE OF REVULSION AND PANIC. HE STAGGERED TO THE BACK DOOR OF THE APARTMENT, OPENED IT UP AND YELLED: "HONEY, COME QUICK, THERE'S A HUMAN LEG COOKING ON THE PATIO GRILL IN THE LEISURE AREA." HE LOOKED OVER AND SAW HIS WIFE, SHE WAS NAKED AND COVERED WITH BLOOD. I DON'T EVEN THINK SHE NOTICED HIM. SHE WAS BUSY HACKING UP FAWN OR SAMANTHA OR WHATEVER HER GODDAMNED NAME WAS, THERE WAS HIS DAUGHTER, IN ZIPLOCK BAGS, IN THE MICROWAVE,

LIQUIFIED IN THE LA MACHINE. SHE SAID: "IT WAS TIME," AND WHAT COULD HE SAY? WHEN THEY HAD GOTTEN HER FROM THE ADOPTION AGENCY, SHE WAS SKINNY AS A RAIL, IT WAS A LOT OF WORK FATTENING HER UP SO THERE WAS SOME MEAT ON THE GIRL'S BONES, BUT THEY HAD DONE IT. HE POPPED A COOL ONE, WANDERED INTO THE LIVING ROOM AND TURNED ON THE TV, MAYBE AFTER THE NEWS HE COULD GET A LITTLE.

. . .

WATCHING THIS DUDE SHOOT UP: I LIKE STICKING NEEDLES IN MY ARM EVERY TIME I DO, I GET HIGH, I FEEL GOOD, I SAY FUCK YOU. WHEN I THROW UP I THROW UP ON YOU. WHEN I NOD OUT, I NOD OUT ON YOU AND YOUR FUCKED UP WORLD. THE TRACKS ON MY ARMS ARE ALL THE TIMES I WON, ALL THE TIMES I SAID FUCK YOU. I LIKE STICKING NEEDLES IN MY ARM! I DO SO MUCH STICKING THAT I DON'T EVEN THINK OF STICKING IT IN. YOU KNOW, I DON'T GET HARD. I DON'T NEED NO

**FUCKING BITCH TO FUCK WITH ME. NO GIRL CAN MAKE YOU FEEL LIKE THIS. I LIKE STICKING NEEDLES IN MY ARM!**

. . .

**THE SIDEWALK SQUIRMS
AND WRIGGLES UNDERNEATH MY FEET
I LOOK INTO THE STREET, IT'S BOILING,
MOVING LIKE A BLACK RIVER
I STEP OFF THE CURB
I SUBMERGE INTO THE ASPHALT
I HAVE BEEN CHRISTENED,
BLESSED INTO THE STREET.**

. . .

**KICKED DOWN THE STAIRS
FELT GOOD TO BLEED
AFTER AWHILE IT HURT SO BAD I WANTED TO KILL
I COULDN'T SEE
ALL THE LIGHTS WERE OFF IN THE BASEMENT
OF LOVE**

. . .

ONE NIGHT I TOOK A WALK DOWN TO THE BEACH TO HEAR THE TEENAGERS ROLL INTO THE SHORE. I SMELLED SMOKE. I LOOKED ACROSS THE STREET TO THE 7-11, SOMEONE HAD NAILED A BUM TO THE NEON LIT 7-11 SIGN, HIS BODY FORMED THE SIGN OF THE CROSS, HE HAD BEEN TORCHED. THERE HE WAS, CRACKLING AND BURNING AGAINST THE NIGHT SKY. HE WAS THE FIRST SAINT I HAD EVER SEEN.

. . .

THERE IS A MAD WOMAN WHO WALKS ALONE DOWN A DARK SIDE OF THE STREET MAKING STRANGE SIGNALS WITH HER HANDS, LOOK AT HER! HER EYES ARE RED AND HER FACE IS GOUGED FROM HER CLAWS, HER GAIT IS PAINED AND LABORED. A LONG TIME AGO SHE DROPPED HER BABY OFF A BRIDGE. SHE IS WRINGED IN GUILT, SHE IS AFRAID, SHE FEELS HATRED. SHE BREATHES IN, SHE BREATHES OUT. FEAR PRESSES ITS COLD HAND ON HER HEART. SHE DOES NOT FEEL IT. SHE REACHES OUT AND CLUTCHES AT THE DARKNESS SHE SMASHES HER FISTS INTO HER FACE WHEN

SHE STARTS TO CRY SHE DISAPPEARS INTO THE DARKNESS / I LOOK OUT MY WINDOW AT NIGHT. UNDER THE STREET LIGHT THERE IS A PACK OF RATS, NOT PEOPLE IN RAT COSTUMES, BUT REAL RATS, THEY ARE CELEBRATING, DANCING IN THE CIRCULAR YELLOW LIGHT THE STREET LAMP CASTS DOWN UPON THE SIDEWALK. THEY ARE IN VICTORY ACTION. THEY KNOW THAT THEY WILL SOON WALK IN BROAD DAYLIGHT BECAUSE ALL OF MANKIND WILL BE DESTROYED / I LOOK OUT MY WINDOW AT NIGHT. ON THE LEDGE ABOVE ME I SPY A PAIR OF SHOE TIPS BALANCING PRECARIOUSLY ON THE EDGE. I HEAR A VOICE, A MAN'S VOICE: "LUCILLE, ARE YOU LISTENING YOU GODDAMNED WHORE? LUCILLE, YOU BITCH I'M GONNA DO IT THIS TIME!" A MAN FALLS PAST MY WINDOW AND LANDS WITH A THUD ON THE SIDEWALK. THERE IS A KNOCK AT MY DOOR. I TURN FROM THE WINDOW. I WALK TO THE DOOR AND OPEN IT, IT'S LUCILLE, SHE'S SMILING.

. . .

I WAS PLAYING AT THIS CLUB IN BIRMINGHAM, ALABAMA, CALLED "THE NICK." I WAS SITTING AT THE BAR STARING AT THE PICTURE OF AMANDA STRICKLAND. I HAD FOUND THE FLYER AT A RESTAURANT A BIT EARLIER THAT EVENING. THE GUY NEXT TO ME SAID "YEA THEY FOUND HER." "IN HOW MANY PIECES? I ASKED. HE SAID "ONE, SHE WAS SHOT TWICE IN THE BACK OF THE HEAD." THE TWO ABDUCTORS HAD HER ABOUT 6 TO 8 HOURS, DROVE HER TO ATLANTA, GEORGIA, KILLED HER AND TOSSED THE BODY. THE BODY WAS FOUND ABOUT TWO WEEKS LATER. THE GUY NEXT ME ADDED: "SHE WAS BI-SEXUAL, YOU KNOW, KIND OF STRANGE. A REAL NICE GIRL."

AMANDA: THE WORLD IS THE PLACE WHERE PEOPLE GO TO DIE.

. . .

ON THE DAY OF OCTOBER 1, 1984 KATHERINE ARNOLD BOUGHT A SHOTGUN AT A K-MART IN LINCOLN, NEBRASKA. KATHERINE, 28, MOTHER OF A SON TOOK

THE SHOTGUN INTO THE PARKING LOT OF THE K-MART, SAT DOWN AGAINST A RETAINING WALL, AND BLEW HER BRAINS OUT. ON OCTOBER 2, I CAME TO LINCOLN TO PLAY AT THE "DRUMSTICK." THE DRUMSTICK IS 100 YARDS AWAY FROM THE K-MART. I SAT MOST OF THE DAY IN THE DRUMSTICK WRITING. NOW AND AGAIN I WOULD HEAR SNATCHES OF CONVERSATION ABOUT HOW "THIS LADY BLEW HER BRAINS OUT." I ASKED THE PROMOTER ABOUT IT, AND HE TOLD ME IT HAPPENED ABOUT 100 YARDS FROM THE CLUB. LATER ON THAT EVENING SOME PEOPLE WERE TELLING ME ABOUT IT, THIS KID CAME UP WITH A McDONALD'S CHEESEBURGER, WRAPPER ALL WRAPPED UP. HE OPENED IT, INSIDE WAS SOME OF KATHERINE ARNOLD'S BRAINS. AFTER THE SHOW I TOOK A FLASHLIGHT AND WENT OUT TO THE K-MART PARKING LOT. I WALKED DOWN THE LOT, PARALLEL WITH THE RETAINING WALL. I SAW CHALK MARKINGS ON THE PAVEMENT, I GUESSED THAT WAS WERE THE MOTORCYCLE HAD BEEN. I MADE A RIGHT AND HOPPED OVER THE WALL, I SHINED THE LIGHT AGAINST

THE WALL. I FOUND THE SPOT. THE WALL WAS TINTED BROWN FROM BLOOD AND GUNPOWDER. THE GRASSY AREA AROUND THE STAIN HAD BEEN CLIPPED. THERE WAS A SLIVER OF BRAIN STILL STUCK ON THE WALL, I PEELED IT OFF. THERE WAS A VERY STRANGE SMELL IN THE AIR. I HAVE NEVER SMELLED ANYTHING QUITE LIKE IT BEFORE. I FELT AROUND IN THE SURROUNDING GRASS AREA. I FOUND SOME PORTIONS OF BRAIN TISSUE. I SAT THERE ALONE WITH THE REMAINS OF K. ARNOLD AND THAT SMELL. IT SEEMED TO BE IN MY PORES, IN MY BRAIN. I REMEMBER GETTING THE FEELING THAT THIS WAS A VERY SPECIAL PLACE, SOME KIND OF HALLOWED GROUND. I WANTED TO STAY LONGER, I WANTED TO SIT DOWN EXACTLY WHERE SHE HAD. AT THIS POINT I WAS OVERCOME BY A FEELING OF BEING WATCHED, WATCHED FROM THE TREES OR FROM SOME PLACE OUTSIDE THE DISTANCE OF THE FLASHLIGHT'S REACH. IT WAS TIME TO LEAVE. I PICKED UP THE PIECES OF BRAIN TISSUE FROM THE GRASS AND WENT BACK TO THE CLUB. WAITING OUTSIDE TO LEAVE, I SAT DOWN AND

THOUGHT ABOUT THE WHOLE THING. AFTER AWHILE, THE BLOOD WOULD WASH OFF THE WALL, THE GRASS WOULD GROW BACK AND IT WOULDN'T LOOK LIKE ANYTHING OUT OF THE ORDINARY. MAYBE SOME KIDS WOULD COME THERE IN A CAR, PARK AND DRINK SOME BEERS, LEGS DANGLING, FEET HITTING AGAINST THE SPOT WHERE KATHERINE ARNOLD'S HEAD RESTED. I WONDERED IF THE PARTYERS WOULD BECOME AWARE OF AN ODOR OF INDESCRIBABLE NATURE. I WONDERED IF THEY WOULD JUST GET UP WITHOUT A WORD AND GET THE HELL OUT OF THERE. I FOUND THE ARTICLE ON KATHERINE ARNOLD IN THE LOCAL NEWSPAPER. I CUT IT OUT, AND DROVE ALL NIGHT TO MINNEAPOLIS.

. . .

KATHERINE, WHO WOULD EVER THINK THAT YOUR TRAIL WOULD END AT K-MART. DID ANYONE TELL YOU? IF YOU WERE ALIVE RIGHT NOW, I MEAN IF YOUR BRAINS HADN'T BEEN BLOWN OUT OF YOUR SKULL WITH THAT SHOTGUN YOU PUT TO IT, WOULD YOU

HAVE BELIEVED THAT YOU WOULD HAVE DONE SUCH A THING? KATHERINE, YOU DID NOT SEE WHAT I SAW. OH GIRL, SOME KID HAD A HUNK OF YOUR BRAINS IN A McDONALD'S CHEESEBURGER WRAPPER, AND WAS SHOWING IT TO PEOPLE. I WENT TO THE PLACE WHERE YOU SHOT YOURSELF, YOU KNOW THE PLACE I'M TALKING ABOUT, YOU WERE THERE BOUT 26 HOURS BEFORE ME. KATHERINE, I SEARCHED THRU THE GRASS WITH MY HANDS, I FOUND PIECES OF YOUR BRAIN COVERED WITH DEAD GRASS AND DIRT. I PEELED A PIECE OF YOUR HEAD OFF THE WALL. YOU MIGHT BE INTERESTED IN KNOWING THAT YOUR HUSBAND FOUND YOU. IMAGINE WHAT HE SAW, YOU WITH NO HEAD, BRAINS ALL OVER THE PLACE. KATHERINE, I HOPE YOU ARE NOT ANGRY WITH ME, I KEPT PART OF YOUR BLASTED UP BRAIN. I WRAPPED IT UP IN A PIECE OF TIN FOIL AND PUT IT IN MY BACK PACK. I THINK ABOUT YOU FROM TIME TO TIME. HEY, YOU MADE THE LOCAL PAPERS AND EVERYTHING. WHO WOULD HAVE THOUGHT YOUR TRAIL WOULD END AT K-MART?

. . .

I JUST GOT OFF WORK. I WORK AT AN ICE CREAM STORE. I SCOOP ICE CREAM INTO CUPS, CONES, PINT CONTAINERS, QUART CONTAINERS, COFFINS AND BODY BAGS. I WORK BEHIND A COUNTER, I'M KIND OF LIKE A BARTENDER. I WATCH THE PRETTY GIRLS PASS THE WINDOW THAT LOOKS OUT ONTO THE SIDEWALK. I'M THE GUY IN THE ICE CREAM STORE. I HAVE BEEN HERE 11 HOURS MY LEGS ACHE. I JUST GOT OFF WORK, IT'S 2:30 A.M. I'M HUNGRY SO I GO TO THE ONLY PLACE THAT'S OPEN. 7-11. I GET THE SAME THING I GET THERE EVERY NIGHT. I SIT ALONE ON THE CURB AND EAT. I HAVE TO WALK TO MY APARTMENT. MY APARTMENT IS HOME. I DON'T WANT TO GO HOME. HOME IS DARK, HOME IS LONELY. HOME IS COLD STORAGE. I'D RATHER GO ALMOST ANYWHERE EXCEPT HOME. I JUST GOT OFF WORK. I SIGNED ON FOR EXTRA HOURS AT THE ICE CREAM STORE SO I COULD HAVE SOMEWHERE TO GO. I GO BACK INTO THE 7-11 TO GET A COKE FOR THE WALK TO THE APARTMENT. IT'S A

**LONG WALK. I DON'T WANT TO GO TO THE APARTMENT. THE APARTMENT KNOWS I'M COMING. THE APARTMENT KNOWS I HAVE NOWHERE ELSE TO GO. THE APARTMENT IS SMILING, IT SHUTS OFF THE HEAT AND WAITS FOR ME TO FALL IN. I LEAVE THE 7-11 AND WALK DOWN WISCONSIN AVENUE, I WALK PAST THE ICE CREAM STORE AND CHECK THE DOOR TO MAKE SURE IT'S LOCKED. I JUST GOT OFF WORK. I HATE MY LIFE. I HATE MYSELF. I FEEL UGLY, UNWANTED, MAD, MEAN, COLD AND CONDEMNED. I MAKE THE WALK TO THE APARTMENT. I PULL OUT MY FOLDING SHOVEL AND DIG DOWN SIX FEET TO MY FRONT DOOR. I JUST GOT OFF WORK.**

**. . .**

**FUCK YOU ALAN:**
**I HAVE BEEN HERE ALL DAY. IT'S SIX PM. I LOOK FORWARD TO GETTING OFF WORK. IT'S COOL NOT TO WORK AT NIGHT FOR ONCE. I GOT NOWHERE TO GO BUT STILL...I'M WAITING ON ALAN TO COME IN AND TAKE OVER. IT'S 6:15, HE'S 15 MINUTES LATE, FUCK YOU ALAN. 45 MINUTES LATER,**

**AT 7:00 PM, ALAN COMES IN, HE IS BLEEDING FROM HIS EYE, HIS FOREHEAD IS SMASHED UP. ALAN ALSO WORKS AT THIS FANCY SHOE STORE UP THE STREET. AT SIX O'CLOCK THE SHOE STORE GOT ROBBED AND THE ROBBER BEAT ALAN'S HEAD IN WITH THE BUTT OF A GUN. ALAN WANTS TO KNOW IF I CAN PULL HIS SHIFT FOR HIM SO HE CAN GO TO THE HOSPITAL. I ASK HIM IF HE IS SURE HE CAN'T WORK, ALAN STARES IN DISBELIEF THAT I WOULD ASK SUCH A QUESTION. ALAN GOES OFF TO THE HOSPITAL IN A CAB. THE NIGHT SHIFT IS HERE. I MIGHT AS WELL BE HERE, I DON'T NEED THE EXTRA MONEY BUT THE STORE BEATS THE APARTMENT, BUT STILL...FUCK YOU ALAN.**

**THIS GUY HAD JUST GOT OFF WORK, HE FELT MISERABLE, IT WAS 3:23 AM. HE WENT**

TO THE 7-11 AND BOUGHT SOME MICROWAVE FOOD. HE SAT OUTSIDE THE 7-11 AND ATE IN SILENCE. HE FELT LOW AND LONESOME, THIS WAS THE USUAL, JUST LIKE THE PLASTIC BAG TASTE OF THE MICROWAVE FOOD, ALWAYS RIGHT THERE. HE THOUGHT OF GIRLS ALOT. ONE IN PARTICULAR. SHE NEVER THOUGHT OF HIM UNLESS SHE NEEDED A RIDE OR SHOULDER TO CRY ON. AFTER HE WOULD FINISH EATING, HE WOULD WALK TO HIS APARTMENT, HE HATED THE APARTMENT, IT MADE HIM FEEL HATEFUL TO BE ALL ALONE IN THERE, IT WAS HARD TO SLEEP IN THE APARTMENT, ALWAYS TOO DAMN HOT, OR TOO DAMN COLD. LOTS OF COUPLES ON THE STREET EARLIER THAT NIGHT. HE WOULD WATCH THEM PASS BY HIS WORK. THEY MADE HIM FEEL UGLY, INHUMAN, LIKE TRASH. HE GOT UP AND STARTED ON HIS WALK HOME. HE HAD TO CROSS A BRIDGE TO GET TO THE APARTMENT. THE BRIDGE WAS VERY HIGH, IT CROSSED OVER A LARGE AND POWERFUL RIVER. ALMOST EVERY NIGHT HE CROSSED THAT BRIDGE HE CONTEMPLATED THROWING HIMSELF OFF.

**THAT NIGHT HE DID, NO REALLY, JUST HOPPED OVER THE RAIL, STOOD ON THE EDGE AND WALKED OFF, NO SHIT.**

. . .

**THE CREW THEY LIVE WAY BACK THERE, SOME WASH DISHES, SOME WORK AT RECORD STORES. THEY DON'T BUM ME OUT. THEY DON'T BREAK MY HEART, THEY DO SOMETHING THAT FALLS SOMEWHERE IN BETWEEN. I FEEL STRANGE AROUND THE CREW SOMETIMES, I FEEL CHEAP, LIKE SOME BIGSHOT THAT EVERYONE HATES. I NEVER WANTED BIG. NO, I NEVER CARED. I WANTED OUT. I LOOKED AT THE BACK OF A RECORD JACKET, I KNEW EVERYONE IN THE PICTURES. I LISTENED TO THE WORDS AS THE RECORD PLAYED, I COULD ALMOST SEE THEM COMING OUT OF HIS MOUTH. I REMEMBER WHEN I WAS IN BALTIMORE LAST. ONE OF THE CREW CAME UP AND SPOKE TO ME, I HAD THESE GIRLS CRAWLING ALL OVER ME AT THE TIME, I FELT LIKE AN ASSHOLE AS I TRIED TO SEPARATE MYSELF FROM THEM. IT WAS HARD FOR ME TO FACE HIM, I DON'T KNOW,**

I FELT LIKE SHIT FOR REASONS I CAN'T EXPLAIN. EVERY OTHER SENTENCE STARTED WITH "REMEMBER," CHRIST I'M ONLY 23. I LOOKED AT THE BACK OF THAT RECORD JACKET AND WROTE ALL THIS. THEY ASK ME WHAT I AM UP TO, I USUALLY LIE, I SAY "NOTHING" SO THEY WON'T ASK ANYMORE QUESTIONS THAT MAKE ME FEEL LIKE A PERSON WHO WON SOME KIND OF PRIZE.

. . .

I WAS AT DISCORD HOUSE IN DC, THE WASHINGTON POST CAME BY TO TAKE PICTURES OF ME FOR AN INTERVIEW I HAD DONE WITH THE PAPER EARLIER. I TOOK THE PHOTOGRAPHER TO IAN'S ROOM SO NO ONE WOULD HAVE TO SEE HIM OR LISTEN TO HIM. HE INSISTED ON GOING DOWN TO THE LIVING ROOM AND TAKING PICTURES OF ME WITH THE REST OF THE GUYS "IN THE BACKGROUND." I FELT LIKE THE BIG SHOT WHO USES PEOPLE HE KNOWS MERELY FOR PROPS. THE PHOTOGRAPHER ANNOYED THE DISCORDIONS, NO FAULT OF HIS REALLY, NO FAULT OF MINE I DON'T THINK. IT MADE ME

**FEEL LIKE I WAS RUBBING SOME IMAGINARY SHIT IN THEIR FACES, IT MADE ME FEEL CRUMMY.**

**. . .**

**ONE DAY, I STOPPED HATING.**
**I CEASED ALL MEANINGLESS ACTIVITY.**
**I COMPLETED THE CIRCLE. I**
**SET MY SIGHTS STRAIGHT. LIKE AN**
**ARROW I FLEW. I STOPPED ACTING**
**I GOT TIRED OF PLAYING WITH YOU.**
**RANDOM VIOLENCE AND DESTRUCTION**
**BECAUSE MY REASON FOR LIVING, MY OUT,**
**MY EXCUSE. WHAT IS YOUR EXCUSE?**
**DESTRUCTION.**
**WITHOUT HATE, WITHOUT FEAR,**
**WITHOUT JUDGEMENT. I AM NO BETTER**
**THAN YOU. NO ONE KNOWS THIS BETTER**
**THAN**
**I DO. I JUST GOT TIRED OF PLAYING**
**PARLOR GAMES.**

**. . .**

**DAVE CLAASSEN ON EXENE:**

"SOMETIMES SHE LOOKS LIKE A WITCH, AND SOMETIMES SHE LOOKS LIKE A TASTY BITCH."

CHUCK DUKOWSKI ON MEXICO:

"WHERE THE AVERAGE DRUNK GOES TO GET DRUNKER THAN AVERAGE."
. . .

LOOK AT YOUR EYES.
YOUR EYES WILL LIE TO YOU
YOU HAVE TO TAKE A WALK IN THE
DESERT. YOU HAVE TO
UNDERSTAND THE WAY THINGS
ARE. YOU HAVE TO TAKE A
WALK THRU THE DESERT.
YOU HAVE TO UNDERSTAND.
WHEN YOU SEE YOURSELF,
MIRRORED IN THE DESERT HEAT,
YOUR EYES CAN NEVER LIE
AGAIN.

EVERY SECOND, I MURDER MY LIFE
I AM ALIVE
I AM SERVING A DEATH SENTENCE

**BORN ONTO DEATH ROW
WALKING AROUND
DANCING ON MY GRAVE**

**BY LIVING, I AM KILLING MY LIFE
DIE, DIE, DIE.
I BREATHE IN
I BREATHE OUT
I AM KILLING, DIGGING A GRAVE,
POUNDING COFFIN NAILS
I'M ALIVE, I'M THE KILLER,
I'M THE VICTIM, I'M ALIVE
. . .**

**THE WORLD IS LAME
PAINFUL, AND HARD TO EXPLAIN.
IN ORDER TO LIVE INSIDE YOUR BRAIN
YOU HAVE TO GO INSANE
YOU HAVE TO DIE
YOU HAVE TO DIE
YOU HAVE TO DIE
DON'T CRY WHEN YOU BID THE WORLD
GOOD-BYE
YOU KNOW YOU HAVE TO DIE TO LIVE IN
HERE
CIRCULAR VISION GAMES BREAKDOWN**

IN CALCULATED PAIN
OH, YOU HAVE TO DIE TO GET BY,
TO LIVE IN THE WORLD'S EYES
YOU HAVE TO DIE
SO YOU CAN LOOK BACK
AND SEE YOURSELF—
WAVE GOOD BYE.

. . .

I PLAYED THIS CLUB IN SAN FRANCISCO. THE NIGHT BEFORE, ANOTHER BAND PLAYED. ALL NIGHT LONG THE GUITAR PLAYER WOULD SIT IN A SMALL ROOM WITH THE LIGHTS OUT. HE SPOKE TO NO ONE. HE PLAYED TWO SETS, HE STOOD IN THE SHADOWS AND PLAYED HIS GUITAR. BETWEEN SETS HE WENT BACK TO THE SMALL ROOM AND SAT IN THE DARK. THE NEXT DAY THEY CLEANED UP THE ROOM, THEY FOUND THE ASHTRAY FULL OF CAMEL NON-FILTER BUTTS, THE ENDS WERE CAKED WITH HEROIN, WHAT A LIFE.

. . .

...HE WALKED DOWN THE HALLWAY, HE STUCK A KEY INTO ROOM 21361. HE SAT

DOWN AT A SMALL TABLE IN THE MIDDLE OF THE ROOM, HE WROTE A SHORT NOTE ON THE BACK OF AN OLD PAPER BAG. IT SAID: "COULD NOT HOLD ON ANYMORE." HE PULLED A .38 CALIBER PISTOL FROM HIS COAT, PUT THE BARREL IN HIS MOUTH AND PULLED THE TRIGGER. "CLICK." NO BULLET. HE FLIPPED THE PAPER BAG OVER AND WROTE "MEMO: BUY BULLETS ON WAY HOME FROM WORK." TOMORROW HE WOULD START FRESH AND GET IT RIGHT.
. . .

LYING IN THE DARK
LYING ON MY BACK
RATS CRAWLING AROUND
BREEDING UNDERNEATH MY SKIN
WAITING ON THAT LAST TRAIN
HEART SLAMMING AGAINST ITS WALLS
BLOOD HURTLING DOWN MY VEINS
WAITING ON THAT PENDULUM BLADE
TO CUT ITS PATH ACROSS MY FLESH
EVERY DAY IT SWINGS A LITTLE CLOSER
AND SOMETIMES I CAN FEEL THE WIND AS
IT PASSES
BY.

...

SHE AND I LAY IN BED
JUST ANOTHER FUCK?
NO!
THIS WAS SPECIAL
BECAUSE I HAD AN AFFECTION FOR HER
SHE GAVE ME HER LOVE
I STUCK IT IN
THEN I TOOK THE KNIFE
FROM UNDERNEATH THE PILLOW
AND I STUCK THAT IN
I SAID "HONEY"
WHICH ONE DO YOU PREFER? SHE DIDN'T REPLY. I GUESS SHE WAS OVERCOME. WHAT KIND OF LOVE IS THIS. IS THIS LOVE? WHAT KIND OF LOVE IS THIS?
...

HONEY, TAKE ME TO YOUR DUMPSTER-BED
FUCK ME HARD ON THE FLY HEAP
WE ARE MONSTERS
WE CREATE MONSTERS
WE MATE AND CREATE
MONSTERS
SLUTS AND KILLERS

**MEAN BLOODSPILLERS**
**WHORES AND FUCKERS**
**FOOLS AND SUCKERS**
**MONSTER FUCKER FATHERS**
**MONSTER SLUT MOTHERS**
**COORS TO YOU REDONDO**
**COORS TO YOU HAWTHORNE**
**INGLEWOOD, THIS BUD'S FOR YOU**
**LAWNDALE, WELCOME TO MILLER TIME**
**SOUTH BAY LOVERS**
**HIDING IN TRASH HEAPS**
**SURFACING TO DUMP TRASH**
**WE ARE MONSTERS**

. . .

**MY EYES ARE TWO SMASHED OUT WINDOWS**
**THRU MY BROKEN GAZE I SEE**
**I STARE AT MY HANDS AND I WONDER**
**WHAT HAS HAPPENED TO ME**
**IT'S SO COLD WHEN THE WIND COMES WHISTLING**
**THRU MY HOUSE**

**MY MIND IS IN THE ATTIC**
**PUSHED ASIDE PILES OF JUNK**
**DARK, CLUTTERED, LOCKED UP**

I CAN'T GET OUT
IT'S LONELY
I'M ALONE IN MY HOUSE

MY HEART IS IN THE BASEMENT
I DON'T DARE COME DOWN THE STAIRS
THE DOOR'S BEEN CLOSED FOR SO LONG
THERE'S SOMETHING DOWN THERE
ITS SO QUIET
NO ONE COMES TO MY HOUSE
. . .

I HEAR VOICES
WHEN NO ONE IS AROUND.
I HAVE SEEN
THE INSIDE OF MY SKULL.
I HAVE CRAWLED INSIDE MY
SKULL. I AM NOT ALONE.
THERE ARE KILLERS IN THERE,
I HAVE MET THEM. SOMETIMES
THEY KICK AT THE INSIDE OF MY
SKULL IT MAKES ME TWITCH
THERE ARE KILLERS LIVING IN MY
SKULL MURDERERS IN MY SKULL
THEY TAKE USE OF MY BODY.
THEY TAKE MY BODY AND

KILL WITH IT. I FEEL NO PAIN
MY BODY IS THE WEAPON OF MY MIND.
I HAVE PRESSED MY HANDS AGAINST
THE INSIDE OF MY SKULL, I HAVE
FELT THE INSANITY. I CAN MUTILATE
I CAN KILL, I HAVE BEFORE, IT WAS
JUST FLESH IN MY HANDS, IT WAS
EASY. I HAVE MURDERERS LIVING IN
MY SKULL. I HAVE MET THEM
FROM TIME TO TIME. THEY ARE MY
FRIENDS, MY TRUE FRIENDS. DON'T
DISTURB MY INSANITY, DON'T YOU DARE.
THERE ARE KILLERS IN THIS HOUSE. THEY
SAY YOU ARE ILL, CURE THE ILLNESS. I
LISTEN TO MY SKULL. I HAVE KILLED
MANY INSIDE MY SKULL. I LIVE WITH
KILLERS. IT IS TIME TO COME OUT.
IT IS TIME TO COME OUT.
IT IS TIME TO COME OUT.
. . .


I HAVE DWELLED IN TOTAL ABSENCE OF
LIGHT. I HAVE BEEN INSIDE MY SKULL. I
WAS NOT ALONE, SOMEONE TOUCHED ME,
I COULD NOT SEE WHO IT WAS. IT WAS
DARK, I COULDN'T SEE HIM. HE WAS COLD.

HIS TOUCH WAS COLD. IT WAS DARK, I COULDN'T SEE WHO IT WAS, I JUST REMEMBER HIS HANDS, THEY WERE COLD, HE SAID "COME HERE, COME HERE, COME HERE," HE WHISPERED, "THERE IS NOTHING TO FEAR. IN DARKNESS, NO FEAR."

. . .

I

THE INSANITY BRINGS MY SOUL TO BOIL, THE INSANITY BRINGS MY BLOOD TO TEARS, THE INSANITY, THE LINES BECOME SO STRAIGHT. I FINALLY UNDERSTAND, MY FRIEND IS HERE, I HAVE FINALLY MET MY FRIEND. NOW I UNDERSTAND EVERYTHING THAT I NEED TO UNDERSTAND. MY FRIEND IS HERE I AM NOT ALONE ANYMORE I'M FREE, MY FRIEND IS HERE. INSANITY.

. . .

II

THE INSANITY IS NO TWISTED BLADE, IT'S LIKE RUNNING YOUR HANDS ALONG A MARBLE PILLAR—COOL, SMOOTH AND RIGHT.

CALMING, LIKE A SANCTUARY FOR YOU**R** WIGGLY BRAIN. I DON'T NEED MY SOUL TIED IN KNOTS THANK YOU, I REMAIN IN THE FIELD OF THE INSANITY, SCOUTING AROUND FOR THE GATE TO INFINITY.
. . .

TALK
LOUD
I NEED TO HEAR IT
I NEED THE COMMAND
I WANT TO HEAR THE COMMAND
I NEED TO HEAR WORDS
GIVE ME THE COMMAND
TELL ME TO SNAP-TO
MAKE ME DO SOMETHING
I WANT THE NEEDLE
I WANT TO HEAR THE NEEDLE
MAKE IT TALK
TELL ME TO VOMIT
THE NEEDLE
I WANT IT IN ME
FUCK ME WITH THE NEEDLE
KILL ME WITH THE NEEDLE
O, NEEDLE, WILL YOU MARRY ME?
I LOVE YOU

YOU
...OMETHING
...IE
KICK ME IN THE ARM
DON'T LEAVE ME
LOVE ME
KILL ME
BUT DON'T LEAVE ME
I WANT YOU IN ME
I LOVE YOU
I WANT YOU IN ME
I LOVE YOU
KICK ME
KILL ME
BUT DON'T LEAVE ME
EVER
. . .

HER SMILE WARMS ME.
IF WE WALKED INTO A
ROOM AND THE LIGHTS
DIDN'T WORK, IT WOULDN'T
MATTER BECAUSE HER
SMILE WOULD LIGHT THE
PLACE RIGHT UP!
I LIVE IN THIS SHED WITH

ABOUT A MILLION SPIDERS
AND SOME ANTS YOU KNOW?
AND EVEN THOUGH SHE LIVES
VERY FAR AWAY, HER PICTURE
HANGS ON THE WALL IN THERE
AND THE PLACE IS NOT SO
BAD, HER SMILE MAKES THINGS
A LITTLE LESS DAMP IN THERE.
I KNOW THIS SOUNDS A BIT DUMB, BUT
SHE IS LIKE A FALL AFTERNOON
AROUND MID-TO-LATE OCTOBER WITH THE
COLD WIND ON YOUR FACE
AND THE LEAVES FALLING
OFF THE TREES AND THAT SMELL IN THE
AIR...
..THAT'S WHAT SHE'S LIKE — GREAT!
AND THAT'S THE WAY I FEEL
ON THAT SUBJECT
. . .

I NOW HAVE YOU STANDING UP. I SLAM MY LEFT FIST INTO YOUR RIB CAGE, THEY EXPLODE UNDERNEATH MY FIST. YOU LIFT YOUR ARMS TO GIVE ME EASIER ACCESS TO YOUR RIBS AND ABDOMEN WHICH I PROCEED TO RUPTURE, YOU SAY "EXCUSE

ME, SIR," AND YOU TURN AWAY AND VOMIT A LARGE QUANTITY OF BLOOD AND MUCUS. YOU WIPE YOUR MOUTH AND APOLOGIZE. YOU STICK YOUR CHIN OUT AND POINT TO IT WITH YOUR BROKEN INDEX FINGER, I OBLIGE YOU BY SMASHING YOUR JAW. I LOOK DOWN, YOU HAVE A LARGE ERECTION, YOU MAKE A SLIGHT PLEADING SOUND AND GESTURE TOWARDS A BASEBALL BAT IN THE CORNER. I BREAK YOUR RIGHT LEG, YOU LAY PRONE WHEEZING. BLEEDING PROFUSELY FROM YOUR MOUTH, YOU ARE CRYING, YOUR TEARS ARE MIXING WITH THE BLOOD AND MUCUS. YOU ARE SAYING SOMETHING LIKE "GASOLINE, THANK YOU SIR; GASOLINE, THANK YOU SIR" YOU EDGE YOUR FACE CLOSE TO MY SHOE YOU ARE ATTEMPTING TO KISS MY FOOT, I WALK AWAY, I COME BACK AND DOUSE YOU WITH A GALLON OF GASOLINE, I AM ABOUT TO STRIKE A MATCH AND THROW IT ON YOU. MORE WHINING SOUNDS COME FROM YOUR MOUTH, SOUND LIKE, "PLEASE SIR, LET ME, PLEASE, PLEASE, PLEASE," I DROP THE BOOK OF MATCHES ON THE FLOOR YOU CLUTCH THEM, STRIKE AND IGNITE.

. . .

**THE BAD LANDS, NEVER TO RETURN, FOREVER LIVING THE END, LEATHER SKIN, ASHES UNDERFOOT, ALL SAINTS FALL BUT NOT NOW, THAT COMES MUCH, MUCH LATER NOW HERE'S A SHOVEL, SOME NAILS, WOOD AND A HAMMER—GO MAKE HISTORY. LEAVE A TRAIL, I DON'T CARE HOW YOU DO IT BUT DO IT. YOU KNOW WHAT I MEAN, I KNOW YOU KNOW. THERE IS NOT THE TIME TO FOOL AROUND. THE CLOWNS DIE. NO MORE BREATHING. WE'RE GONNA MAKE IT OH SO HOT ASHTRAY LIFE, ASHES, ASHES OH SO HOT, INCINERATION. WE CAME TO THE END, WE FOUND NOTHING, NOTHING!!! AND WE CURSED BECAUSE WE WERE HOPING FOR SO MUCH LESS**

. . .

**I AM A FOOL, EVERY NIGHT I WANT TO DIE. I THINK HOW GREAT IT WOULD BE TO BE TORN LIMB FROM LIMB BY THEIR GREEDY LITTLE HANDS, TO BE KICKED INTO THE GRAVE BY THEIR DIRTY FEET. TORN TO BITS. WHEN THEY DESTROY ME, THEY**

**DESTROY THEMSELVES, I'M EASIER! SO LET IT BE! I LIKE IT, I LOVE IT! YOURSELF YOU'RE LOVING ME. WHEN YOU KILL ME, YOU'LL DIE A THOUSAND TIMES. THAT'S THE ONLY REASON THAT I'M HERE, FOR YOUR LOVE. NOW DIG: I REVEL IN MY STUPIDITY. I WALLOW IN MY MORTALITY. THE COWARDS OF THE WORLD COME TO ME FOR PRO TIPS! I'M THE KING OF FOOLS WITH NOTHING TO PROVE, AND EVERYTHING TO LOSE. NOW IF YA THINK YA LOST IT ALL, YOU'RE WRONG, YOU CAN ALWAYS LOSE A LITTLE MORE, SO COME ON, GET ON UP, RISE UP! HEY GIRLS, HEY! COME ON DOWN AND LOSE. RIGHT HERE, RIGHT HERE IN THE HERE AND NOW. WE'RE NAKED IN THE EYES OF TIME SO COME ON, WRAP YOUR MIND AROUND MINE LOOK INTO MY EYES AND LIE A THOUSAND TIMES AND DIE A THOUSAND MORE. IF A COWARD DIES A THOUSAND TIMES, THEN I HAVE NEVER LIVED. I'M TOO BUSY DYING TO EVEN BREATHE.**

. . .

**OPEN THE DOOR**

**PUT ME IN AN APARTMENT**
**MAKE IT CRY**
**MAKE THE WALLS CONVULSE**
**LOOP THE EXTENSION CORD**
**AROUND THE LIGHT FIXTURE**
**DO IT FOR ME**
**I CAN'T DO IT MYSELF**
**I'M HELPLESS**
**I NEED YOU TO HELP ME**
**I'M CALLING OUT TO YOU**
**I NEED YOU**
**I NEED HELP AND ASSISTANCE.**
**PUT THE CHAIR UNDERNEATH THE LIGHT**
**HELP ME DIE**
**I CAN'T DO IT MYSELF**
**HELP ME DIE**
**I WANT YOU TO WATCH**
**HELP ME**
**PLEASE HELP ME**
**DON'T LEAVE ME**
**TELL ME TO GET ON THE CHAIR**
**PUT THE CORD AROUND MY NECK**
**DON'T LET ME DOWN**
**I'M COUNTING ON YOU**
**I NEED YOU**
**HELP ME**

**TELL ME TO GET UP ON THE CHAIR**
**GOOD**
**PUT THE CORD AROUND MY NECK**
**I WANT YOU TO WATCH**
**PUSH ME OFF THE CHAIR**
**I'M HANGING, I'M SWINGING**
**I'M DOING MY TIME**
**I'M DOING MY TIME**
**I'M DOING MY TIME**
**I'D WHISTLE YOU**
**A TUNE BUT MY**
**TONGUE IS TURNING BLACK**
**AND IT'S SWELLING**
**UP**
**MY HEAD FEELS LIKE IT'S GOING TO EXPLODE**
**ARE YOU WATCHING, I CAN'T SEE YOU**
**MY EYES ARE RIVETED TO THE CEILING**
**MY THROAT IS THRUST FORWARD, EXPOSED**
**MY THROAT IS SHINY WITH OILY SWEAT**
**CUT IT**
**GET A KNIFE AND CUT MY THROAT**
**CUT IT**
**DISEMBOWEL ME**
**TAKE THE KNIFE**
**AND CUT MY STOMACH OPEN,**

**GRAVITY WILL
CAUSE MY GUTS TO
FALL ALL OVER THE
CHAIR AND THE FLOOR.
(I GOT GUTS, SEE?)
NOW LEAVE ME
LEAVE ME
LEAVE ME
TURN THE LIGHT OUT
LEAVE ME
REMOVE YOURSELF
CUT AND STICK
CURE THE ILLNESS
CLOSE YOUR EYES
CLOSE YOUR EYES
DON'T COME BACK
DON'T COME BACK
DON'T COME BACK
CLOSE THE DOOR
CLOSE THE DOOR
CLOSE THE DOOR
GIVE THE KNIFE
TO THE GIRL IN
MY DREAMS, TELL
HER ABOUT THE
LONG NIGHTS. TELL HER**

**ABOUT THE SELF
INFLICTION, TELL HER
TO CUT ME DOWN
TELL HER TO CUT ME DOWN
AND I'LL FALL
RIGHT INTO HER ARMS.**

. . .

**SHE GOES TO THE 7-11. SHE BUYS A SIX PACK OF MILLER (HIGH LIFE), A BOX OF TAMPONS AND A PACK OF CIGARETTES. SHE WALKS HOME TO HER DINGY ROOM SHE RENTS AT THE EDISON HOTEL. SHE SITS AND DRINKS AND SMOKES AND BLEEDS AND WATCHES THE SUN GO DOWN. IT HURTS TO BE ALONE WHEN IT'S COLD OUTSIDE. IT HURTS TO BE ALONE WHEN IT'S COLD INSIDE. IT HURTS TO BE ALONE WHEN IT HURTS TO BE ALONE.**

. . .

**SEEN TOO MUCH
HIT TOO HARD
TOO MUCH DAMAGE
JUST IMAGINE SOMEONE WALKING**

**AROUND SMOLDERING FROM AN O.D. OF LIFE**
**A WALKING WRECK**
**A PATHETIC SHELL**
**WHAT I FEEL**
**PAIN, DEPRESSION**
**I'M TIRED**
**I DON'T WANT TO REACT**
**I'M WRECKED**
**PULL ME OFF TO THE**
**SIDE FOR A BREATHER—WHAT DO YOU MEAN THERE'S NO TIME?**
**. . .**

**SITTING ON THE STEPS AT 7-11 EATING MY BURRITO AND BIG GULP THINKING OF WHERE I'M GOING TO SLEEP TONIGHT. I JUST GOT OFF WORK AND I'M STILL TENSE BUT COOLING OUT ON WISCONSIN AVE. IS MAKING ME UNWIND A LITTLE, OCCASIONAL CAT CALLS FROM CARS NO SWEAT. I GOT MY CAR, I THINK I'LL SLEEP IN FRONT OF IAN'S HOUSE BECAUSE I GOT SPOOKED REAL BAD LAST NIGHT IN THAT PARKING LOT. NICE NIGHT BREEZE TONIGHT, THE AIR SMELLS GOOD. I LIKE IT OUT HERE.**

HANGING OUT WITH NATHAN IN BACK OF THE 7-11 ON CONNECTICUT AVE. I GOT A BURRITO AND A BIG GULP, NATHAN, HE LIKES THAT HIPPY GIRL WITH THE BIG TITS AT WORK. WE BOTH WORK AT THE SAME PLACE. YEA, JUST SITTING THERE UNWINDING AND ENJOYING THE COOL NIGHT AIR IT'S NOT TOO LATE TO US — 3:30 AM, THE NIGHT IS STILL YOUNG IF YOU DRANK 8-9 COKES AND ATE YOUR FILL OF ICE CREAM AND NUTS, I FEEL AS IF I HAVE BEEN WORKING THIS JOB FOR A LONG TIME. I FEEL BURNED OUT AND RELIEVED THAT MY SHIFT IS OVER.

. . .

I'VE GOT AN ALIENATION
I GOT AN ALIENATION
SITTING RIGHT HERE
MY FRIEND AND ME
I'M ALL THE WAY ALONE
HAND IN HAND WITH ME
IN MY ALIENATION
IN THE DESERT OF MY ALONITY
I'VE GOT A BLACK HOLE

**SO DEEP AND DARK**
**I LIVE THERE**
**INSIDE MY BLACK HOLE SOUL**
**WHERE YOU CAN'T GO**
**WHERE YOU CAN'T SEE**
**WHERE YOU CAN'T HURT ME**
**ANYMORE**
**I'M LIVING IN MY ALIENATION**
**I'VE GOT AN ALIENATION**
**. . .**

**I WAS RUNNING ON THE STRAND DOWN NEAR THE HERMOSA BEACH PIER. IT WAS A CLEAR DAY. EVERYBODY WAS OUTSIDE. I SAW ALL THESE PEOPLE IN SHORTS AND BIKINIS, HAVING BEERS, PLAYING VOLLEYBALL ON THE SAND, RUNNING AROUND, LAUGHING, CALLING OUT TO EACH OTHER, COOKING HAMBURGERS ON HIBACHIS, PLAYING ZZ TOP, FOOLING AROUND ON SKATE BOARDS, BEAUTIFUL GIRLS, ALL TANNED AND SLIM, SMILING AND TALKING WITH GUYS, PEOPLE GETTING DRUNK—TALKING LOUD AND LAUGHING LIKE A BUNCH OF HYENAS—MIGHT HAVE BEEN NICE TO HAVE BEEN PART OF IT.**

I SAW THIS GUY WALKING DOWN THE STREET WITH THIS GIRL. THEY WERE BOTH SMILING, THEY WERE HOLDING HANDS. YOU KNOW SHE WAS ONE OF THOSE BLONDES, AND SHE HAD THESE NICE CLOTHES ON, AND THEY WERE LAUGHING AND TALKING JUST WALKING DOWN THE STREET, PROBABLY GOING TO EAT DINNER AND THEN GO TO A MOVIE OR A PLAY...I WOULD HAVE TRADED PLACES WITH THE GUY IN A SECOND.

. . .

I WAS IN THIS APARTMENT IN THE EAST VILLAGE. I SAW THIS GUY SHOOTING UP HEROIN. HE TIED OFF HIS LEFT ARM WITH AN EXTENSION CORD. HE PUT THE NEEDLE IN HIS ARM. THE BLOOD WENT UP THRU THE NEEDLE AND MIXED WITH THE HEROIN. HE HAD HIT THE VEIN. HE SHOT THE HEROIN AND BLOOD MIXTURE INTO HIS ARM. HE RELEASED THE EXTENSION CORD AND PULLED OUT THE NEEDLE. HE BENT FORWARD AND VOMITED ALL OVER HIS LAP. HE LEANED BACK AGAINST THE WALL. A

TRAIL OF SPITTLE CAME FROM HIS MOUTH ONTO HIS SHIRT. HIS ARM WAS BLEEDING, I NOTICED BLACK AND BLUE BRUISES FROM WHERE THERE WERE PREVIOUS NEEDLE PUNCTURES. HE DIDN'T BOTHER TO WIPE UP THE BLOOD, VOMIT OR SPITTLE, HE SEEMED UNCONCERNED. HE SEEMED HAPPY. I DON'T KNOW, SEEMED KINDA NICE.

. . .

I GOT A DESERT IN MIND AND I GO TO GET LOST BECAUSE I'VE BEEN FOUND TOO MANY TIMES BEFORE, SUNRISE BURNING BRIGHTLY, BURNING EYES INTO THE BACK OF MY HEAD, LIKE I SAID I'VE BEEN FOUND BEFORE WHEN I'D THOUGHT I'D LOCKED THE DOOR. I'LL STEP BEHIND THE BLINDS OF MY MIND AND WALK ALONG THAT LONELY DESERT ROAD. TALKING ABOUT MY ONLY TRAIL, MY ONLY FRIEND, LIKE ANY DESERT SCENE. I HAVE COME TO COMPLETE THE CIRCLE, I HAVE COME TO COMPLETE THE CIRCLE. I HAVE COME TO COMPLETE THE CIRCLE. WHEN I AM DONE I WILL BE ONE, IN DEATH I WILL BE ONE. I

AM A SNAKE THAT HAS BEEN STEPPED ON, LYING SCATTERED SHATTERED AND FORGOTTEN ON THE SIDE OF A TRAIL. SQUIRMING SEVERED I FEEL NO PAIN, JUST THE HEAT OF THE SUN AND THE CRAWLING FAMINE THAT IS MY NAME.

. . .

I AM MY END
I AM MY END
I AM THE CRAWLING FAMINE
I AM MY END

. . .

I'VE GOT A PLACE
I'VE GOT A DESERT
I'VE GOT A GOOD THING GOING
DON'T CLIMB DOWN HERE
YOU PUT ME ON THE OUTSKIRTS OF TOWN
NOW YOU WANT IN?
YOU THINK YOU DO.
I'LL TURN YOUR LIGHTS OUT
I'LL TAKE YOUR VIRGINITY AWAY AGAIN
CAN
YOU
DIG

**IT?**
**I LIVE IN A HANGING GARDEN**
**SUSPENDED FROM YOUR WORLD**
**IN ALIENATION: NO SEARS AND ROEBUCK**
**DREAMS**
**NO CREDIT IS GOOD**
**IN ALIENATION: I AM WHOLE**
**COMPLETE**
**THE FULL CIRCLE REALIZED**
**IN ALIENATION**
**IN THE ALIENATION**
**IN THE PEACE OF 21,361 MINDS**
**IT'S ONLY COLD IN YOUR WORLD**
**WHEN I'M WITH YOU I'M COLD.**
**ALIEN**
**YOUR WORLD IS SUCH A LONELY PLACE**
**WHEN I AM THERE**
**I AM COLD**
**YOU ARE A BAD TRIP**
**THAT'S WHY I QUIT YOU**
**THAT'S WHY I SPAT YOU OUT**
**THAT'S WHY I WENT UP RIVER**
**INTO THE DESERT**
**INTO THE JUNGLE**
**INTO THE SUN**
**I EXIST IN ALIENATION**

**I AM NOT ALONE
I AM JOINED BY THOSE WHO KNOW THAT PARADISE
LIES
. . .**

**BY DECEMBER 27, THE DEAD HAD STARTED TO FILL THE STREETS. I STEPPED AROUND THE CORPSES ON MY WAY BACK FROM 7-11. ON THE AFTERNOON OF THE 28TH THE REFUSE TRUCK CAME TO PICK THEM UP. THE BODIES WERE SO EMACIATED THAT THE WORKMEN COULD PICK THEM UP AND PITCH THEM INTO THE TRUCK WITHOUT ANY TROUBLE. WHEN THE TRUCK BED WOULD FILL TO THE TOP, IT WOULD BE DRIVEN TO THE OUTSKIRTS OF TOWN. THE BODIES WOULD BE DUMPED INTO A LARGE PIT AND INCINERATED. THIS WAS AN EFFICIENT METHOD OF DISPOSAL. BY JANUARY 2, A FEW MORE BODIES HAD BEEN DRAGGED OUT OF THE HOUSES AND DEPOSITED IN THE STREETS. THERE THEY LAY MIXED IN WITH COORS LIGHT CANS AND USED CONDOMS. THEY WOULD SOON BE HAULED AWAY AND INCINERATED. BY JANUARY**

**THIRD THE STREETS WERE CLEAR. ALL THE CHRISTMAS TREES HAD BEEN REDUCED TO ASH.**

. . .

**I'M LOOKING THRU THE WINDOW AT THESE GUYS SITTING AT A BAR. THEY STARE INTO THE DARKNESS, THEY SMOKE, THEY DRINK THEY TRY NOT TO EXIST, THEY DRINK AND CURSE AND BURN AND WEEP AND DRINK AND HATE IT, AND DRINK AND GRIND THEIR TEETH, AND DRINK AND WRING THEIR HANDS AND DRINK AND LIVE A SLOW LIFE-LIKE DEATH AND DRINK AND SINK INTO THEIR STOOLS.**

. . .

**I AM THE INCINERATION MAN. A DISCIPLE OF THE SUN. I'M YOUR MAN. I DON'T WANT TO WASTE YOUR TIME. I DON'T WANT TO TAKE YOU JUST ANYWHERE, I WANT TO TAKE YOU NOWHERE. I'VE GOT A MAGIC TOUCH. BLOW OUT THE CANDLES ON YOUR BIRTHDAY CAKE, GET IN THE CAR, WE ARE GONNA FLAME BROTHER.**

. . .

TAKE A WALK ALONG BUT NOT ALONE.
TAKE ME WITH YOU
PLEASE
UNRAVEL, UNFURL, COME UNDONE
PLEASE
OPEN THE CURTAINS OF YOUR HEART
LET ME SEE INSIDE
YOUR THEATRE
I WANT A FRONT ROW SEAT WHEN THE MOVIES
START ROLLING
NO
I WANT TO TOUCH YOU
BUT I CAN'T
NOT WITH THESE DESPICABLE HANDS
MY HANDS ARE UGLY
OFTEN WASHED, BUT NEVER CLEAN
THE FILTH IS BELOW THE SKIN
I WANT TO SEE YOU
I CAN'T LOOK AT YOU FOR TOO LONG, YOU MIGHT
NOTICE ME
THIS WOULD BE A DISASTROUS THING
MY EYES ARE UGLY
I DIDN'T KEEP THEM CLOSED ENOUGH

I LOOKED AT THINGS TOO CLOSELY
I DON'T TOUCH, I DEFILE
PLEASE DON'T LOOK AT ME
I DON'T LOOK, I STARE
I MUST GO NOW
WATCH ME SCURRY AWAY
. . .

I'M WALKING ON A TIGHTROPE
THEY SAY
IF I KEEP STRAIGHT I'LL COPE
I CAN'T MESS UP

THEY TOUCH ME AND I SCREAM
THEY TELL ME TO LIVE
THEY TELL ME HOW
I CAN'T GO ON LIKE THIS

I WANT TO LIVE
I WANT TO LIVE
I DON'T WANT IT TO BE TAKEN AWAY
I KNOW THEY HAVE PLACES FOR PEOPLE
LIKE ME

THIS CAN'T BE THE ONLY WAY
JUST TO EXIST ON A TIGHTROPE

**I'M NOT LIVING
I'M ALREADY DEAD INSIDE**

**NO, NOT AGAIN
I CAN'T GO THROUGH IT
I THINK TOMORROW IS GOING TO
BE TOO MUCH.**

. . .

IT IS PAINFULLY SIMPLE TO UNDERSTAND. YOU'RE GONE, AND I MISS YOU. I THINK I HAVE DIED A FEW TIMES SINCE YOU'VE BEEN GONE. I WISH YOU WOULD COME BACK TO ME. I LIE AWAKE AT NIGHT AND THINK ABOUT YOU. I FEEL LONELY. I FEEL WEAK. YOU'RE GONE AND I MISS YOU. I FEEL LIKE I WANT TO DIE. YOU'VE HEARD THIS BEFORE IN A MILLION SONGS, I KNOW, BUT MY ROOM HAS TURNED INTO A PENITENTIARY. IT'S COLD AND I GOT RINGS UNDER MY EYES BECAUSE I DON'T SLEEP GOOD ANYMORE. I KNOW I SOUND LIKE A PATHETIC FOOL BUT I CAN'T HELP HOW I FEEL RIGHT NOW. SEE? I'VE BEEN HURTING MYSELF AGAIN. THE PAIN TAKES MY MIND OFF THE HURT. GIRL, I MISS YOU

**SO BAD I DON'T KNOW WHAT TO DO WITH MYSELF. I DON'T KNOW WHAT TO DO.**

**PLEASE COME BACK, PLEASE?**

**. . .**

**IT'S DECEMBER 24, 1984, CHRISTMAS EVE. I ALWAYS SPEND THESE JOLLY TIMES IN PLACES WHERE THE LONELY AND FORGOTTEN TYPES SEEM TO GRAVITATE. LOOK AT THOSE BROKEN FACES IN THE DINER WINDOW, MELTING INTO THEIR COFFEE CUPS, CIGARETTE SMOKE CURLING UP AROUND THE SOCKETS OF THEIR DEAD EYES. MERRY CHRISTMAS DEAD MAN. IT'S THE TIME OF THE SEASON TO BE WITH FAMILY AND FRIENDS, I LOOK AT THE PEOPLE SITTING IN THE BAR, GETTING NUMB, TOASTING THEIR LONELINESS TO THE WINKING CHRISTMAS LIGHTS STRUNG UP AROUND THE MEN'S ROOM. BACK A FEW YEARS AGO I CAN REMEMBER SITTING IN MY APARTMENT ALONE ON CHRISTMAS EVE, WATCHING THE CARS PASS BY MY WINDOW. I WAS FEELING MIGHTY LOW, NOWHERE TO GO, I DIDN'T KNOW WHAT I HATED MORE,**

HAVING NOWHERE TO BE OR FEELING THAT I HAD TO BE SOMEWHERE. OH MAN, LOOK AT THOSE PEOPLE AT THE GEORGETOWN THEATRE ON WISCONSIN AVENUE! A GUY PAYS HIS $3.50 AND SITS THRU 4 TO 5 SHOWINGS OF THE FILM SO HE CAN HEAR SOME VOICES OTHER THAN THE ONES SCREAMING IN HIS HEAD. I AM WISHING THAT THE ICE CREAM STORE THAT I WORK AT WAS OPEN SO I COULD GO AND DO A SHIFT, TURN ON THE RADIO AND FORGET MYSELF IN THE FLUORESCENT LIGHT. CHRISTMAS EVE IS HERE AND THE COLD STOVE IS BURNING. I HEAR SOMEONE SAY "PETER LAWFORD, THE ACTOR DIED, HE'S BEEN DYING FOR 20 YEARS" I'VE BEEN DYING FOR 23.

. . .

THEY GO AROUND AND AROUND
THEIR HEARTS BEAT
THEY LIVE
THEY EXIST
BUT THEY DON'T KNOW WHY
EVERYTHING THEY KNOW (WE KNOW)
IS A MATTER OF FACT

**INSTINCT
DRIVE
THE NEED TO SLEEP
BUT THEY DON'T KNOW WHY
FROM START TO FINISH
THEY DON'T KNOW WHY
INSTINCT DRIVES TO SURVIVE
BUT THEY (WE) DON'T KNOW WHY**

. . .

**IN BEAUTIFUL REDONDO BEACH ON ARTESIA BLVD. RIGHT NEAR THAT 7-11. THAT'S WHERE THE PINKHOUSE LIVES. CHEAP SHIT PLASTER, LAUGHING CAR SALESMEN, SHADE TREES. THE NIGHTS ARE HOT AND FULL. NO ONE WILL HEAR YOUR SCREAMS WHEN YOU ARE SLAUGHTERED IN THE BACK ROOMS OF THE FILTHY PINK HOUSE.**

. . .

**THE MAN LIKED HIS UNIFORM. HE LIKE THE WAY IT LOOKED IN THE MIRROR. HE LIKES WHAT IT DID TO PEOPLE. HE GOT OFF ON THE FEAR AND HATRED AND JEALOUSLY IN THEIR EYES. HE LIKED TO TOUCH HIS GUN. HIS GUN FELT GOOD, HARD, COOL, AND**

SMOOTH. HE DIDN'T LIKE GIRLS. HE ONLY GOT HARD WHEN HIS UNIFORM WAS ON. THAT GUN FELT SO GOOD. HE NEARLY SHOT A MAN ONCE. A FUCKING NIGGER. HE COULDN'T PULL THE TRIGGER. HIS HAND WAS SHAKING TOO MUCH. HE COULD NOT COME FOR WEEKS AFTERWARD. HE CAME HOME ONE EVENING AND STOOD IN FRONT OF THE MIRROR. HE COULDN'T GET HARD, HE TRIED DIFFERENT POSES, WITH HIS SUNGLASSES ON AND OFF, NOTHING. HE CLOSED HIS EYES AND STROKED HIS COCK AND REMEMBERED THAT NIGHT THE SUMMER BEFORE WHEN HE HAD THAT MAN FACE DOWN ON THE SIDEWALK. HE HAD THE GUN AT THE DUDE'S HEAD. MAKE ONE MOVE YOU PIECE OF SHIT AND I'LL BLOW YOUR FUCKING BRAINS OUT. HIS HAND HADN'T SHOOK HE WAS HARD IT FELT GOOD, SO GOOD. STILL NO ERECTION, IN A FLASH HE WAS DOWN ON HIS KNEES, THE BARREL SLIDING IN AND OUT OF HIS MOUTH, SO HARD, SO SMOOTH. THE GUN CAME IN HIS MOUTH.

. . .

I AM SITTING AT THE BAR, I AM HAPPY, DRINKS ARE 1/2 PRICE, IT'S HAPPY HOUR. I'M WATCHING THE GAME ON TV. ALL MY FRIENDS ARE HERE. BOY ARE WE GETTING FUCKED UP. I HAVE ENOUGH COURAGE TO KIND OF FLIRT WITH THE BARMAID. SHE CAN'T SEE HOW MY STOMACH FOLDS OVER MY BELT, THAT PARTICULAR VIEW IS OBSTRUCTED BY THE HEIGHT OF THE BAR. I CALL HER "BOO-BOO," SHE CALLS ME "YOGI." I THINK SHE LIKES ME. SHE TALKS ABOUT THIS SINGER NAMED PRINCE SOME NIGGER ON MTV. I'LL BUY HER SOME COKE, SHE MIGHT FUCK ME THEN. I HAVE A WIFE MAYBE BY THE TIME I GET HOME THE OLD BITCH WILL BE ASLEEP AND I WON'T HAVE TO LOOK AT HER. I YELL AND LAUGH WITH MY BUDDIES AS WE WATCH THE GAME, "YEA, LOOK AT THAT NIGGER RUN, LOOK AT 'IM!" I AM JEALOUS OF THE FOOTBALL PLAYERS. I CAN'T PLAY SO I JUST DRINK BEER AND WATCH, I AM PATHETIC, I AM STUPID, I AM DRUNK, I AM FAT AND FUCKED UP. I SHOULD BE DESTROYED.

. . .

TO FIND THE TRUTH, YOU HAVE TO L.I.E. THE BIG TRUTH IS THE BIG LIE. WHEN YOU SEE THE TRUTH YOU'LL KNOW WHAT I MEAN. THE TRUTH EXISTS IN A LIE. THE TRUTH IS A LIE. L.I.E. -- LIVING IN EXILE. TO TELL THE TRUTH, YOU MUST LIE. THE TRUTH IS TOLD WHEN YOU ARE ALONE. THE TRUTH IS ADMITTING TO LIES, ISN'T IT?

. . .

THE DESERT IS ON FIRE. THE DESERT IS BURNING FOR ME. SPIRITS RISING OUT OF THE GROUND. WHEN I SAY THAT THE DESERT IS ON FIRE, I MEAN TO SAY THAT THE DESERT IS ON FIRE! I MEAN TO SAY THAT I AM ON FIRE. I'M STANDING UP, WALKING AROUND AND BURNING DOWN. I AM INCINERATING. THE DESERT IS BURNING, THE SPIRITS ARE RISING OUT OF THE GROUND. THE SNAKES AND THE SPIDERS AND THE VULTURES AND ALL THE OTHER SISTERS AND BROTHERS ARE ON FIRE, IT'S US. WE ARE BURNING. AT THE END WE ARE PAINLESS, CHARRED, BLACK AND SILENT.

. . .

I DID A SHOW IN KANSAS CITY. AFTER THE SHOW I WENT WITH THE PROMOTER TO HER CAR THAT WAS PARKED AT A BAR NEXT DOOR. THERE WAS A BAND PLAYING INSIDE THE BAR. YOU COULD HEAR THE BAND, THEY WERE PLAYING "SHAKIN' ALL OVER" ... "C'MON, CLAP YOUR HANDS, I CAN'T HEAR YOU!" A CAR PULLED INTO THE PARKING LOT, THREE YOUNG MALES GOT OUT, THEY WERE PRETTY BIG. ONE SAID: "YA THINK THERE'S ANY FAGGOTS IN THERE?" ONE OF THE OTHER TWO SAID: "IF THERE ARE, WE'LL KICK THE SHIT OUT OF THEM." THEY WALKED INTO THE BAR.

. . .

I'VE SEEN MOD SQUAD. THAT GUY WAS ON DRUGS. HE TRIED TO FLY OFF OF A ROOF, I WASN'T BORN YESTERDAY, I READ NATIONAL GEOGRAPHIC, I READ TIME, I KNOW WHAT'S GOING ON, I WAS IN THE BIG ONE, I WASN'T SCARED -- I KNOW WHATCHA THINKIN' I KNOW WHATCHA THINKIN' YOU'RE SAYING -- THIS GUY'S A SAP, HE WAS PROBABLY BORN YESTERDAY! HEY, I'M NO

**CHUMP, I WASN'T BORN YESTERDAY, I KNOW WHAT THOSE KIDS ARE SMOKIN', I'VE SEEN NEGROES, NOT JUST IN PICTURES PAL! I'M STREET WISE, I KNOW MY WAY AROUND, I'M NOT GONNA FALL FOR THAT "HEY SIR MAY I HOLD YOUR WALLET FOR A SECOND?" CRAP, WHAT'S THAT? HEY I WASN'T BORN YESTERDAY, I'M NO FOOL, I DON'T TRUST ANYONE NOT EVEN MY WIFE, I LEARNED THAT IN PRISON, WELL IN A MOVIE ABOUT PRISON BUT I WATCHED IT AND TOOK NOTES. I BEEN AROUND, I KNOW ABOUT CONTRACEPTIVE DEVICES I KNOW WHAT GOES WHERE, I KNOW WHAT GOES WHERE, YOU DON'T HAVE TO TELL ME, I'M NO FOOL, I WASN'T BORN YESTERDAY!**

...

When I was 19 I worked for awhile at a lab facility in Rockville, Maryland. The place had mice, rats and rabbits. I was a drone. Mondays I mopped the facility, Tuesday I loaded dirty cages into a huge washer. Wednesday, Thursday and Friday would pass in similar fashion. One day whilst transferring the 300th batch of mice into a clean cage,

Mike, the head man came into the room. He told me that there was an outbreak of rodent disease called ectromelia throughout the entire facility. All the animals in the facility were to be destroyed and incinerated.

Mike -- "Henry, do you want to do it, I mean would it make you squeamish?"

Henry -- "No, hell no."

Mike -- "You'll do it?"

Henry -- "Sure."

Fine. By order of the National Institute of Health (N.I.H.), 15 to 17 thousand little beasts were to be destroyed. Fine, clean their cages, mop their floors, sterilize their rooms, now I got to kill them, fine. Most of the staff was relocated to another facility, it was me and the animals pretty much. I had a room all empty and waiting. I was to gas them. The procedure was simple enough, I would put 20 to 30 animals in a glad bag, squeeze the air out, stick in the gas tube, turn on the gas.

Fine. I would go into the rooms and pull out the carts that held cages, I would wheel the cages into the death room. I had the bags and the gas tank of CO2. I would kill, cage by cage, when the boxes would fill up with dead rats and mice, I would take the boxes over to the big N.I.H. facility where I would incinerate them. From 7:30 in the morning, until 4:30 in the evening, I killed them. Each time I would gas, I watched the animals die. When the mice would be put into the bag, they would crawl around, sniff and try to figure out what they were doing there. Then when I would stick the tube in and turn the gas on, they would leap up the sides of the plastic bag as it ballooned full of the gas, they looked like they were jumping for joy or something. They would fall back down to the bottom, gasping, soaking in their own urine. They always died with their eyes open -- always. I would look thru the bag and look at their eyes, their bodies stacked in a heap. The bottom of the bag was always warm from their piss and shit. I would tie the bag off and throw it in a specially marked box. That sound, I'll never forget that sound, the gas hissing, and the scratch of the little claws scurrying up the inside of the bag. They always died the same, wide-eyed and with no idea why. I was Adolph Eichmann, I was ordered to terminate. I was not a murderer, I was just trying to get the job done with maximum efficiency. I would terminate and incinerate. I like the way that sounds. Yes, I brought them to the camp in carts that held up to 2,000 at once, efficient. I gassed them in enclosures, that contained the bodies, their wastes and their disease. Efficient! The corpses were taken to the ovens and incinerated, leaving behind disease-free ashes, efficient. They called me a murderer. A saint maybe, a murderer, no. After all, it was I who cured the illness. It was I who stopped its spread. I destroyed the ill and the weak, those who were not fit for survival. Can't you see? I did a job that had to be done. I tried to give rise to a strong, perfect, disease-free race and you call me a criminal? I am a humanitarian in the strongest sense of the word.

Inside of a week and a half the facility was silent. All were incinerated, except for one load that I dumped in Burger King and 7-11

dumpsters. I quit the month after and started working in an ice cream store. A while ago, I was thinking that it would have been alot more fun to distribute the boxes in more interesting locales. How about taking boxes of dead mice and rats to a nice residential neighborhood and putting a box on each doorstep? How about ups'ing a whole bunch to your old high school or girlfriend's house. You could open up the boxes and bomb people on the sidewalk. How about taking a bag, putting it on someone's doorstep, lighting the bag on fire and ringing the doorbell. The guy comes out and stomps the fire out and ... gross -- rodent flambe underfoot! You could freeze 'em and throw them at people in Westwood -- fun!!! With an open mind, the possibilities are endless.
. . .

KEEP ME PREOCCUPIED
KEEP ME BUSY, BUSY, BUSY
SO I WON'T HAVE TO THINK
I DON'T WANT TO THINK
BECAUSE IT ONLY BRINGS ME PAIN
I JUST KEEP RUNNING AWAY FROM
MY PROBLEMS

KEEP ME BUSY
GIVE ME A MILLION THINGS TO DO
SO I CAN KEEP RUNNING AWAY
FROM MYSELF.
. . .

BLACK:
THE COLOR OF SILENCE
THE COLOR OF PEACE
THE COLOR OF THE EARTH
BURNED TO A CRISP
THE COLOR OF DEAD, CHARRED
BODIES
BLACK:
THE COLOR OF PEACE
THE COLOR OF NO PAIN
THE COLOR OF NOTHING
NOTHING!
THE END OF WAR
THE END OF HATE
THE END OF NOISE
BLACK:
THE COLOR OF INFINITY
THE COLOR OF ALIENATION'S VACUUM
THE COLOR OF INSANITY'S DREAM
THE COLOR OF REALITY'S NIGHTMARE

**THE COLOR OF THE FULL CIRCLE REALIZED ULTIMATE FINAL HARMONY.**

. . .

**SUNDAY AFTERNOON DEIRDRE & I WERE EATING AT BIFF'S ON WILSHIRE BLVD. IN SANTA MONICA. I WAS FINISHING 2 EGGS & TOAST WHEN A PURSE SLAPS DOWN ON MY SEAT. I LOOK OVER, THERE IS THIS OLD LADY WITH HER PANTS DOWN TO HER KNEES, FLASHING ME TWO STICK LEGS AND DIRTY BROWN UNDERWEAR. SHE SAYS "MY PANTS ARE FALLING DOWN GIRLS." DEIRDRE SAYS: "PLEASE! YOU'RE EMBARRASSING HENRY!" THE LADY, SEEING THAT I'M NOT A GIRL YELLS: "DON'T LOOK!" DON'T LOOK? I WISH I WAS BLIND! I JUST FINISH EATING AND SOME OLD CREEPY LADY COMES OUT OF NOWHERE AND DROPS HER DRAWERS IN MY FACE. I NEED THIS?**

. . .

**PRO TIPS FROM ROLLINS**

1. Do not have the girl meet you at the pet shop that you work at. You are covered with lice, mites, ticks and cat hair, and you smell like a litter box!

2. Do not be going to an all-boys school for the last 1,2,3,4,5 years and had ridlin tablets shoved down your throat for the last 8, makes you act all weird and shit.

3. There are lots of things not to say, for example: "So what is your history class like?" "Skateboard much?" "Maybe you can come over to my house sometime and I can show you my snakes and rats and my tarantula!"

4. Your attire is of the utmost importance. Please do not dress in a yellow t-shirt, light blue Levi cords, and brand new never-been-worn iridescent white sneakers. You'll glow in the dark, stop cars, and look like a total asshole.

Remember how clean your face has been for the last few months? Never fear, Friday morning you will wake up with 3 to 5 large,

**cancerous zits on your face. Right, O.K. settle down.**

**5. Be careful when you select the movie. If it's too boring or something, your date will excuse herself and go to the lobby. You figure that she is going to the ladies room or something. Twenty minutes later, interest piqued, you venture into the lobby to see what is going on. There is your date, she's standing by the cigarette machine talking to a guy with stubble, sideburns and a football jacket. He's got twenty pounds and seven inches on you. His shoes don't glow, and he stares at you while you blush. "Oh, he is in my acting class" you find out later.**

**6. Now your stomach is starting to churn. You have to take the girl home and kiss her goodnight. No, this is not the fiftieth girl you have gone out with, you're not trying to see if you can get her pants off on the first date. You are wondering just how you got yourself into this mess in the first place, and how you are going to make it thru this alive. Oh, you hope:**

"Unkissed virgin and date die in public transit crash, details at eleven" Yeah, please don't cover your fear with pseudo-cool moves and casually spit on the ground, miss, and have to wipe it off her bare leg with your yellow t-shirt. You are now at the front door, don't faint or vomit you're going to be alright.

7. You are not kissing your aunt or your granny, this is a human being! Wait at least one to two extra seconds before you say, "Good night, I had a really good time, maybe we can go out again sometime." You're suppose to put your tongue in and roll it around like you are an expert, which you will be on Monday morning when your friends ask you what happened.

8. Always lie. "What happened? What happened? I got attacked is what happened! That girl was all over me. I had to peel myself off to beat the milkman home!" and your friends will all nod their heads with understanding, for they too pecked their date

on the lips and made it home at 10:15 p.m., just like you.

. . .

The boy turned fifteen. His father bought him a 20-gauge shotgun. He taught his son how to load, how to clean and how to shoot the gun. He would say kid: "You've got to stand up for yourself always." He would make the boy shoot round after round, his shoulder would ache. He would rather read comics and masturbate like a normal boy of his age. He didn't like going to the rifle range with his father, the place gave him the creeps. One Saturday morning in August, his father said "Get your rifle and get in the car, move it." He did what he was told. He sat in the front seat waiting for his father, dreading another 4 hours of shooting. His father got in the car, they drove to the railroad tracks down by the river. They got out. "Where are we going dad?" The boy asked. Dad said nothing and gestured to the underpass of a bridge that went over the tracks. There was a bum sleeping in a gully near one of the bridge supports. The father put his hand over his mouth to signify that he wanted quiet. He handed the boy a round, the kid loaded it into the rifle. "When I was your age, my first hit was a deer but times have changed." He walked over to the bum and kicked him soundly in the ribs, the bum screamed and tried to get up. "Shoot him!" Yelled dad. The kid just stood there. "I said shoot him!" The bum was now on his feet and pleading for his life. The kid started to shake and dropped the rifle. The bum tried to escape, the shot caught the bum right in the cheek, removing most of his face and forehead. He grabbed the kid by the arm and walked him over to the corpse. He pushed the kid's face an inch away from the bum's shattered face. "Look! Look! You little coward, look!" The boy was crying, he tried to cover his eyes but his father grabbed his arms. Finally he grabbed the boy by the hair and took him back to the car. Father and his son the wimp, went home.

. . .

WALKING DOWN ARTESIA BLVD. I WALK PAST THIS SOUPED-UP CHEVY. THERE'S A MAN INSIDE. HE IS LYING IN THE BACK

SEAT. HE LOOKS LIKE A CORPSE, ARMS FOLDED ON HIS CHEST, BASEBALL CAP OVER HIS FACE, I BREATHE-IN HIS AFTERSHAVE AND KEEP WALKING.
. . .

PHONE CALLS, FRIENDS, VALENTINE'S DAY CARDS, CATS, PARTIES AND THE COUNTLESS GAMES THAT MAKE PEOPLE HURT, CRY, LAUGH, ETC. THESE THINGS ARE HANDS THAT STICK OUT THE WINDOW AND CATCH YOU AND BREAK YOUR FALL AFTER YOU THROWN YOURSELF OFF THE ROOF. THE SOUND OF THEIR VOICES, THE PAIN THEY INFLICT, THE GAMES THEY PLAY, THE NOISE, THE NOISE, KEEPS YOU FROM GOING INSANE. THEY KEEP YOUR MIND OFF YOUR MIND. DOWN THE ROAD APIECE IN THE HOUSE OF THE ALIVE, THERE IS DARKNESS, SILENCE. YOU CAN HEAR THE WATER DRIPPING OFF THE ROOF OF YOUR SKULL. THERE'S NOTHING THERE TO STOP YOU FROM HEARING THE SILENCE. YOU WISH FOR A PHONE CALL, A HUMAN TOUCH, ANY NOISE WILL DO. BUT IT'S TOO LATE. YOU KNOW TOO MUCH. YOUR EARS TURN

**DEAF TO THE NOISE. JUMPING OFF THE ROOF AND THE BOTTOM IS BECOMING CLEARER.**

. . .

**THEY WERE CLEANING UP THE PLACE, IT LOOKED LIKE A PARTY THAT HAD GONE TOO FAR, LOOKED LIKE A GARBAGE DUMP. BODY BAGS FOR THE WHOLE ONES, AND GLAD BAGS FOR THE PARTS. CUSTODIANS CLEANING UP, PICKING UP LIMBS, GUT, BODIES, YOU COULD SMELL THE SEMEN, BLOOD, AND BURNED FLESH. EVERYBODY WAS DEAD. LUGGAGE, BODY BAGS AND CUSTODIANS LUMBERING AROUND, STEPPING OVER CHARRED CORPSES.**

. . .

**SHE HAS SEEN PEOPLE SHOT DOWN IN THE STREET, IMPRISONED IN DEATH CAMPS. SHE HAS SEEN STARVATION AND UTTER HOPELESSNESS OF SURVIVAL. NOW SHE WANTS WARMTH, PEACE AND QUIET. SHE HAS LIVED IN DAYS OF PAIN, DARKNESS, COLD AND DEATH. WHEN SHE SMILES, IT'S FOR REAL.**

. . .

**I WAS IN MY CAR, PARKED OUTSIDE DUNKIN' DONUTS JUST GOIN' OUT OF MY FUCKIN' HEAD MAN, NOT LAUGHING OR CRYING OR ANYTHING MAN, FEELING NOTHING! JUST FREAKING OUT OF MY HEAD. I COULDN'T FEEL A FUCKIN' THING, DIDN'T KNOW WHO I WAS OR WHAT I WAS, OR IF I WAS AT ALL. I WAS FREAKING OUT TOTALLY.**

. . .

**I LOOK ACROSS THE WAY. I SEE THAT MAN IN HIS ROOM-CELL. BLUE LIGHT FLICKERING THRU THE WINDOW. ALL THE LIGHTS ARE OFF. JUST THAT BLUE LIGHT FLICKERING, BLINKING, WRAPPING TIGHT. O, HE'S GOT THE BLUE LIGHT ON. HE'S GOT THAT BLUE LIGHT ON. HE'S TURNING COLD BLUE. LIGHTS OFF. HE'S COLD WHEN THAT BLUE LIGHT'S ON. HE SITS ALONE IN THE DARKNESS, HIS FACE REFLECTING THE COLD BLUE LIGHT.**

. . .

SLEEP TIGHT. I HOPE THAT NOTHING COMES AND STEALS YOU AWAY IN THE NIGHT. I HAVE MANY FROZEN MILES TO TRAVEL BEFORE I SEE YOUR EYES AGAIN. I NEED TO SEE YOUR EYES SLEEP TIGHT, I'LL REACH YOU IN YOUR DREAMS, REACH OUT AND CATCH ME, PULL ME DOWN, I'VE LOST MY WAY.

. . .

SATURDAY AFTERNOON, NBC WIDE WORLD OF SPORTS. FILM OF MEN IN KAYAKS PADDLING DOWN WHITE WATER RAPIDS, BEAUTIFUL, SUNNY MOUNTAIN FOOTAGE. THE ANNOUNCER CUTS IN: "SOME PEOPLE WILL DO ANYTHING TO GET TO THE GREAT OUTDOORS!" SCENE CUTS TO BLACK AND WHITE FOOTAGE OF THE BELSEN DEATH CAMP IN GERMANY. MEN ARE PITCHING DEAD BODIES INTO THE BACK OF A WIDE BODY TRUCK. ONE OF THE MEN TURNS TO THE CAMERA, WAVES AND SMILES.

. . .

A JOB WORTH DOING IS A JOB WORTH DOING WELL, SO THEY SAY. EFFICIENCY

AND FRUGALITY ARE VIRTUES IN ANY AGE. YOU WORK HARD FOR THE BOSS. YOU PLAY BALL FOR THE COACH. PULL FOR THE HOME TEAM. BE TRUE TO YOUR SCHOOL. KEEP YOUR EYES AND EARS OPEN AND YOUR MOUTH SHUT. LOOK OUT FOR NUMBER ONE. BE STRONG. STRIVE FOR PERFECTION IN EVERYTHING YOU DO. PEOPLE WHO DO WHAT THEY ARE TOLD CAN BE MOST TERRIFYING.

. . .

ANCIENT INDIAN TRIBES IN CENTRAL AMERICA USED TO HAVE HUMAN SACRIFICES. THE HIGH PRIESTS WOULD CUT OUT THE HEART OF THE SACRIFICED AND EAT IT. THEY WOULD PROBABLY CALL US VIOLENT AND PRIMITIVE FOR THE WAY WE LIVE TODAY. I WOULD HAVE TO AGREE.

. . .

FUCK THIS, I JUST WANT TO GET THE JOB DONE. I CAME HERE TO GET THE JOB DONE! FUCK THIS SINCERITY BULLSHIT! TONS OF PEOPLE ARE SINCERE, COPS ARE SINCERE, SO WHAT! I COME TO GET THE

**JOB DONE, LIKE H&R BLOCK, LIKE HITLER, LIKE GOD, LIKE U2, LIKE 7-11, LIKE THE PEACE CORPS, LIKE A QUASI-COMMUNAL-CO-OP ANARCHOSYNDICATED ART-COLLECTIVE, MAN.**

. . .

**WALKING AMONG THE HANDSHAKERS. WATCHING THEM FEED, BREED, KILL AND SHAKE HANDS. WATCHING THEM WATCH ME. I WANT TO BE A PENDULUM BLADE, SWINGIN' AND A'KILLIN' AND A'SLASHIN' DOWN THE WAY. STAMPING THEM OUT LIKE CIGARETTES.**

. . .

**WHEN WE ARE LYING NEXT TO EACH OTHER, I LOOK AT HER NAKED BODY. I TRY TO IMAGINE SOMEONE ELSE ENTERING HER, KISSING HER. I TRY BUT I CAN'T, I CAN, BUT I CAN'T REALLY.**

. . .

I'm at the D.D. sitting at the counter with my coffee and cornbread muffin. I watch the people come in and out. A man and his young daughter come in and get some milk and donuts. The place is pretty much empty. For some reason the little girl plops down on the stool right next to me. The father takes a look at me, I smile. He says to his daughter, "Come on honey, let's sit at a booth, there's a lot more room." No way, the kid likes it right here, with me. I don't know why, but it's kind of fun to see dad squirm a bit for his toasted coconut and milk. "C'mon honey, let's go," dad says. He shoots another glance my way, of course I'm smiling! Hey Dad, I like kids, no really. Finally she gets off the stool. She waves at me and smiles, I wave back to dad. At the next counter over, two young college type males are talking, they sit with a stool in-between them. They might as well be a city block apart. What is that shit, what are they afraid of? Dunkin' Donuts is a place where a man can hang his hat, where a man can choose his own destiny, caffeinated or decaffeinated.

. . .

**HERE IS SOMETHING TO DO -- GO INTO A 7-11, ANY 7-11. POSITION YOURSELF IN A**

**PLACE WHERE EVERYONE CAN SEE YOU AND SCREAM:**

"I AM ADOLF HITLER! I AM ADOLF HITLER! THE NEXT PERSON WHO DRINKS FROM THE DE-CAFFEINATED COFFEE POT IS GOING TO GET THEIR ARM RIPPED OFF AND FED TO THEM! DO I MAKE MYSELF PERFECTLY CLEAR?"

**THEN TURN AND MOONWALK OUT THE DOOR.
BELIEVE ME, IT'S COOL.**

. . .

I was at Deirdre's house, Deirdre was asleep and I was sitting in the living room. There was a knock at the door. It took me a minute to get the door open with the locks and all. I opened the door. A man and a woman stood before me. The girl started first.

"Hi, we're on a tri-national door-to-door raffle sweepstakes lottery for Southern California, don't worry, we're not moonies!"

I stared at the rose in her hand and wondered why I was being put thru this.

"Where are you from?" she asks.

"The other side of town."

"The other side of the country? I'm from Maryland, my name's Tina, what's yours?"

"Henry."

"Andy? Well, hi Andy, this is Damien."

"Hi Damien."

"Hi Andy!"

"Well, can you help us win?" Tina asks.

"What do you want me to do?"

"Buy a magazine."

"I don't want a magazine."

"Ok, well 'bye Andy!"

They turn and leave and I call after them --

"Hey, you should invest your winnings in bullets and shoot pigs."

They left real fast, it was cool.

. . .

Yes it was Saturday night, yes it was raining, yes he was alone and yes, he was bored. Bored, but not crazy. He sat at the kitchen table fiddling with a common kitchen knife. Just for something to do, he started whittling the index finger of his right hand. "Pretty keen!" He muttered. He proceeded to whittle off the remaining digits of his right hand. In the space of half an hour he had carved his entire right arm off to the shoulder. The phone rang, he put the knife down and picked it up, it was Ed, his buddy from work -- "Yeah, what's up, Ed?"

"I was thinking how cool it would be to go get a couple of sixes and climb the water tower and spray paint our names on the water tank and climb back down like we did last week."

"No thanks, Ed."

"I've got all the "Friday the 13th" movies on one video cassette, we could sit up all night and watch them again."

"'Bye Ed."

Ed was crazy.

He hung up the phone and picked up the knife, he started on the toes of his right foot. He worked away until there was no leg left. He did the same to the left leg. He sat there with the knife, staring at his cock. No, he wasn't going to cut that off. He was bored, hell yes, but not crazy.

. . .

I saw the Rock Awards on TV last night. Now those people are just ridiculous. Giving a trophy out for music. What do you do with it? Put it on the mantle next to your bowling trophy? They had a few of the artists perform live, one of them was Prince. Is this guy for real? I thought he was going to cry. He kicked over the mike stand dude, probably ruined the $300+ sennheiser cordless mike, hey man, this is rock and roll and we don't care, not us hell no. Ok fine. They gave out trophies for best male video. The choice was between Prince & Bruce Springsteen. I forget who won, but it would have been more fun if it was a tie and the Boss & Prince duked it out on stage, I think Springsteen would have kicked Prince's purple butt all the way back into the Warner Bros'. Main office dude hey I saw John Cougar bone Huey in the butt while the news looked on. I tell ya, this rock and roll biz is tough stuff, living on the edge all the time, I mean would you, could you live in Motley Crue's stack heels for a day? Probably not. Hey look, let's have lunch, I want to give you my new video cassette, could you give me yours? Great! Maybe my bodyguard can exchange video cassettes with your bodyguard at lunch and we wouldn't have to bother. OK, I'll have my bodyguard's agent give your bodyguard's agent a call and they can set up a meeting thru their respective record companies. They can do an album together, and a video. What were we talking about?

. . .

I HAVE SEEN YOU THROW PEOPLE AROUND AND SHIT. THE ONES THAT ENJOY THEIR WORK ARE THE ONES THAT THIS LITTLE MISSIVE CONCERNS. I SAW THIS SHOW IN THE SUMMER OF 1981; THE BOUNCERS HAD BEEN A BIT OVER THE TOP THAT NIGHT. WELL, HERE IS THE FUNNY PART. ONE OF YOU BOYS WAS GOING TO HIS CAR TO DRIVE HOME. ONE OF THE "BOUNCED" WALKED UP AND SUNK AN ICE PICK INTO THE BOUNCER'S SIDE, ALL THE WAY, UP TO THE HANDLE. I, OF COURSE THOUGHT THIS WAS COOL. A FEW WEEKS AFTER THAT, A HIGHWAY PATROL PIG WAS BLOWN OFF HIS BIKE BY A SHOTGUN BLAST. THIS BROUGHT A SMILE TO MY FACE AGAIN. I THOUGHT ABOUT YOU BOYS AND HOW EVERY ONCE IN A WHILE YOU GET IT. IT WILL HAPPEN AGAIN, YES IT WILL, NEXT TIME IT COULD BE YOU. WE CAN ONLY HOPE.

. . .

THERE'S A CRAZY MAN WITH
VACUUMS IN HIS EYES
HE SAYS HE CAN HEAR THE SUN RISE
HE SAYS IT MAKES HIM A BIT OFF BALANCE
HE SAYS IT MAKES HIS SOUL SCREAM
NOW ALL THE CITIES BURN DOWN
IN THE SLUMS AND THE GUTTERS
OF HIS MIND
AND HIS DREAMS
ALL THE CITIES BURN DOWN
DOWN THRU THE TIMES
OF HIS CHILDHOOD MEMORIES
THAT STRUCK AND STRIKE AND IGNITE
WITH BURNING PAIN
NOW BURN DOWN
THE CITIES BURN DOWN
HE CLOSES HIS EYES
AND THE CITIES BURN TO THE GROUND
THE STREETS ARE FULL OF ASHES
HE WALKS ALONE
HIS EYES PULL IN THE WIND
AND THE ABANDONMENT OF
EVERY CITY
THAT PASSED THRU HIM
AND LEFT HIM COLD

HE CLOSES HIS EYES
AND THE CITIES BURN DOWN
. . .

LIFE'S ABANDONMENT IS PAINLESS
LIFE'S ABANDONMENT IS SILENT
THE ABANDONMENT GROWS INSIDE
LIKE A FREEZING, KILLING, CRAWLING
CANCER
BORN, AND LEFT IN THE DUST
THE SUN COMES UP
YOU'RE WALKING DOWN THE STREET
YOU REALIZE THAT YOU HAVE BEEN LEFT
IN THE HOUSE ALL ALONE
IT'S COLD INSIDE
THE DOORS ARE LOCKED
YOU'RE NEVER COMING OUT

WHO LEFT YOU?
NO ONE LEFT YOU
YOU'RE LOOKING AT YOURSELF
AND THERE'S NOTHING WRONG
YOU'RE LOOKING AT YOURSELF
AND THERE'S NO ONE HOME INSIDE
YOU SAY "HEY WHERE HAVE I GONE?"
YOU WENT NOWHERE

**THAT'S THE ABANDONMENT**
**I OPEN MY EYES AND I SEE IT**
**I FEEL IT**
**IT CONSUMES ME**
**THAT'S THE ABANDONMENT**
**TURN ME OFF**
**OR CUT ME**
**TURN ME OFF**
**OR CUT ME**
**TAKE MY MIND OFF MY MIND**
**. . .**

**I WAS STANDING ON THIS BRIDGE THAT CROSSES OVER FOUR LANES OF TRAFFIC. I WAS STANDING THERE, SWEARING, MINDING MY OWN BUSINESS, THE USUAL. THIS KID COMES UP TO ME, HE SAYS: "HEY MISTER, HAVE YOU SEEN A BROWN AND WHITE DOG GO BY?" I SAID "FORGET THE DOG, KID, GET UP ON THE RAIL HERE." I PATTED THE MARBLE GUARD RAIL WITH MY HAND. THE KID GOT UP ON THE GUARD RAIL AND LOOKED DOWN AT THE WHIZZING TRAFFIC BELOW. "NOW JUMP" I SAID. THE KID JUMPED OFF. HE FELL ONTO THE ROAD AND DIED. STUPID KID.**

. . .

COME HOME
CLOSE THE DOOR
LOCK THE DOOR
MAKE SURE YOU LOCK THE DOOR
PULL BACK THE CURTAINS
LOOK OUTSIDE
THE STREETS ARE FULL OF KILLERS
THE STREETS ARE FULL OF KILLERS
SNAKES AT YOUR FEET
FEEL THE DIRT TOUCH THE DISEASE
CURE THE ILLNESS
STOP THE HURT
CURE THE ILLNESS
STOP THE HURT
CURE THE ILLNESS
STOP THE VISION
STILL THE TURBULENCE
SIT DOWN ON THE COUCH
TAKE A LOAD OFF
TAKE OUT THE GUN
PUT THE BARREL IN YOUR MOUTH
PUT THE BARREL IN YOUR MOUTH
CLOSE YOUR EYES
THINK OF THE FILTH,

**THINK OF THE ALIENATION
THINK OF THE ALIENATION
BECOME THE ISOLATION
EMBODY THE ALONE
USE IT AS A WEAPON
ALIENATE OTHERS
FROM YOURSELF
FROM THEMSELVES
USE THE WEAPON
PULL THE TRIGGER
SHOW THEM WHAT YOU'RE MADE OF
SHOW THEM WHAT YOU'RE MADE OF
STOP FLAILING AROUND
PULL THE TRIGGER
END THE JOKE
END THE JOKE
MAKE IT REAL
END IT
END IT
END IT
. . .**

**I'VE GOT A FRIEND
I'VE GOT A FRIEND
ON A TRAIL THAT NEVER ENDS
I ONCE TRIED**

TO DIE INSIDE HER EYES
UNTIL I FOUND OUT
THAT SHE HAD GONE BLIND
NOW ALL SHE SEES
IS THE DARKNESS OF HER MIND
I'VE GOT A FRIEND
. . .

I AM IN MY SHACK
IN THE BACKYARD
A LITTLE BIT OF SUNLIGHT
YOUR SUNLIGHT
FILTERS THRU THE WINDOW
IT GIVES ITSELF SILENTLY
WALKS RIGHT THRU THE WINDOW
FROM YOUR WORLD
INTO MINE
. . .

THE WORLD CAN BE SUCH A COLD AND LONELY PLACE. THIS IS SOMETHING THAT EVERYBODY KNOWS. SO COLD AND DARK THAT SOMETIMES I THINK I'M GOING TO DISAPPEAR AND GO SPINNING DOWN THE DRAIN. DOWN TO SOME COLD SEWER. SELF-DESTRUCTION BECOMES A STRAIGHT

LINE. STRIKING BACK AT A WORLD THAT DOES NOT EVEN KNOW YOUR NAME. YOU CAN'T HURT IT, IT CAN ONLY HURT YOU BACK.

. . .

WHEN I'M DOWN IN THE SUBWAY
WHEN I'M DOWN IN THE SUBWAY
TRYING TO FIND MY WAY
DOWN IN THE REFRIGERATION MIND
DOWN IN THE BASEMENT OF MY ALIENATION
I SEE HER FACE
I SEE HER FACE
COMING THRU THE WALLS
SHINING
DOWN ON ME.

. . .

THE BABY WAS BORN, IT WAS SLAPPED. THE BABY STARTED TO SCREAM. THE GREASY, BLOODY BABY MADE A LUNGE, THREW ITSELF BACK ONTO THE GURNEY WHERE ITS' MOTHER LAY. THE BABY TRIED TO CRAWL BACK INSIDE THE MOTHER. THE CHILD'S OILY FINGERS CLAWED, STRAINING ITS HEAD FORWARD. THE DOCTOR

GRABBED IT BACK INTO HIS HANDS. THE BABY SCREAMED, "NO!" THE DOCTOR WAS SO SHOCKED THAT HE NEARLY DROPPED THE CHILD. THE CHILD WAS WASHED AND PUT IN THE MATERNITY WARD WITH THE REST OF THE INFANTS. LATER THAT DAY, A NURSE FOUND THE CHILD, COLD, BLUE, DEAD, ITS LITTLE HANDS WRAPPED AROUND ITS OWN THROAT.

. . .

WHEN I DIE, BURY ME IN THE BACKYARD OF THE GINN'S. IT'S REALLY NICE BACK THERE, THE YARD IS COVERED WITH CLOVER AND PINE NEEDLES. THERE IS AN OLD GREY CAT THAT HANGS OUT, THERE IS A NICE OFFSHORE BREEZE. IT'S QUIET, NOBODY IS EVER BACK THERE EXCEPT FOR ME. WRAP THE BODY UP IN A SHEET, DIG A HOLE AND THROW THE BODY IN, COVER THE CORPSE WITH DIRT, GO BACK INSIDE AND WATCH BENNY HILL.

. . .

A BUM STOOD AT THE LUCKY MARKET RIGHT IN FRONT OF ARTESIA & BLOSSOM.

HE WAS BEGGING FOR MONEY. HE LOOKED PRETTY PATHETIC, DRESSED IN RANCID, OILY CLOTHES. HE SMELLED LIKE CIGARETTES AND URINE. "CAN YOU SPARE A DIME?" HE WOULD ASK. PEOPLE WOULD SHAKE THEIR HEADS OR WALK WAY AROUND HIM. HE WAS GETTING NOWHERE. TWO HOURS WENT BY, NO MONEY, NOT A CENT. "PLEASE, A DIME!" CRIED THE BUM. A MIDDLE AGED MAN WALKED BY HIM, HEARD HIS PLEA AND LAID UPON HIM A MINT NEW DIME FROM HIS PANTS POCKETS. "THANK YOU, SIR! THANK YOU!" SHOUTED THE BUM. A DIME IN HAND, THE BUM LIMPED OVER TO A PHONE BOOTH AND CALLED IN THE AIR STRIKE.

. . .

I'LL BE BACK IN A LITTLE WHILE, I'M GONNA GO DOWN TO THE STORE, THEN I'M GONNA GO SHOOT MR. T. I'M GONNA SELL ALL THAT GOLD AROUND HIS NECK, GONNA BUY ME SOME DRUGS, GONNA BUY ME SOME GUNS, GONNA BUY ME SOME BULLETS, GONNA SHOOT EVERY PIG I SEE GONNA WATCH THE PIGS GET SHOT DOWN TO THE

GROUND. PIGS, DYING, SQUEALING, BLEEDING LIKE STUCK PIGS. THE ONLY WAY THEY KNOW.

. . .

SHE'S KIND OF DRUGGY. ON AGAIN OFF AGAIN. THE TIMES WHEN SHE'S ON, SHE'S ON, SHE'S BUMMING ON HAVING TO COME DOWN, WHEN SHE'S OFF, SHE'S TALKING ABOUT GETTING ON. SHE'S NOT AN ADDICT, IT'S AN ON AGAIN/OFF AGAIN KIND OF THING, YOU KNOW, LIKE THOSE "HEROIN WEEKENDS" PEOPLE GO FOR, METH RUNS ETC., YOU KNOW WHAT I'M TALKING ABOUT. SHE PULLS AN APPLE CART, THE DRIVER HAS A STICK WITH AN APPLE ON A STRING, HE DANGLES IT IN FRONT OF HER NOSE. SHE SEES A SYRINGE, THE NEEDLE SHINES, SHE LIKES THE WORD "SPIKE" THE NEEDLE IS A LOVER, SHE LIKES THE WORDS "DOING A DIME" THE NEEDLE IS BOSS, THE NEEDLE IS HER BEST FRIEND. IF SHE SAYS "TIE ME OFF, LOVER" ONE MORE TIME, I'LL SCREAM, I SWEAR.

. . .

**HER EYES**
**HER TOUCH**
**HER VOICE**
**TAKES MY BREATH AWAY**
**SHE'S NICE ENOUGH**
**TO GIVE IT BACK**
**THANKS FRIEND**
**I NEEDED THAT**
**. . .**

**I'M SWINGIN' A NOOSE WRAPPED AROUND MY NECK. THE ROPE IS TIED TO THE SKY. I'M FLOATING THRU THE AIR, DEAD. PEOPLE LOOK UP IN THE AIR AND SEE MY DEAD, BLOATED BODY PASS. TWO LOVERS ARE LYING IN THE DIRT, PUSHING EACH OTHER AROUND, THEY LOOK UP AND MY EYES MEET THEIRS, BURNING DOWN THE WORLD. THE TWO LOVERS START MAKING ANIMAL SOUNDS. THEY SINK THEIR CLAWS INTO EACH OTHER'S FLESH AND FUCK UNTIL THEY ARE LOVELESS, BREATHLESS, SEXLESS AND ALIVE, THEY SAY "THANKS DEAD MAN!" OH, MY DEATH IS A TURN ON! I MADE THE WORLD CRY, SHUDDER AND CRACK. I MADE THE FLOWERS BURST INTO FLAME,**

FLOATING ALONG, TURNING EVERYTHING ON. I AM BLACK AS ANY DEAD SUN, SHINING DOWN A DEAD LIGHT TO MAKE IT ALL COME ALIVE AND BURST INTO FLAME HANDLING DOWN A DEAD LIGHT, LIKE A MESSAGE. FIRING DOWN A DEAD LIGHT. O,
THEY SEE ME COMING ON A HARVEST WIND
THEY SEE ME BURNING HOTLY
THEY SEE ME SHINING BLACKLY
THEIR LUNGS FILL WITH FIRE
AND THEY EMBRACE EVERY BREATH
LIKE A DEAD FRIEND
COME BACK
TO LIFE.
. . .

A RAT WENT INTO A HOLE IN THE WALL.
HE TOOK A SHARD OF GLASS
HE SLASHED HIS OWN THROAT
HE CLUTCHED THE SHARD OF GLASS IN HIS GREASY LITTLE MITTS
AND CARVED A REAL SMILE
INTO HIS THROAT
GUESS HE COULDN'T
TAKE THIS SHIT ANYMORE
. . .

I AM THE BUBONIC PLAGUE
I TURN YOU BLACK
I MAKE YOU DROP AND DIE
I FILL YOU WITH PAIN
I MAKE YOU CONVULSE AND SCREAM
THEY BURN YOUR CORPSE
I AM THE RATS
I AM THE GREY WIND
I AM A SEX MACHINE
I FUCK YOU SLOW
I FUCK YOU ALL
I FUCK YOU TILL YOU DIE
I HAVE BEEN GONE FOR A LONG TIME
BUT IT'S TIME FOR ME TO COME
BACK. I SEE THE PIGS, I SEE
THE KILLERS, I SEE THE ALIENATION.
YOU FEEL SUPERIOR TO THE VERMIN
YOU NEED TO FEEL SUPERIOR TO THE VERMIN.
YOU NEED TO FEEL SUPERIOR TO THE VERMIN.
YOU CALL THE PIGS ON THE VERMIN, YOU CALL
THE EXTERMINATOR ON THE VERMIN. I AM A

SUPERHERO. I AM THE DIVINE PUNISHMENT!
I
AM GOING TO DESTROY YOUR LIFE. I AM GOING
TO TERMINATE YOUR EXISTENCE THOROUGHLY,
UNBIASEDLY, YES.
I'M NOT RACIST
I AM NOT SEXIST
I HAVE NO POLITICAL LEANINGS
I'M NOT IN THIS FOR THE MONEY
THIS IS THE BEST DEAL YOU EVER HAD
I DO NOT HATE!
. . .

THEY ARE AT A BAR. THEY ARE SITTING AT A TABLE, THE WAITRESS COMES OVER TO TAKE THEIR ORDER. SHE ORDERS A DRY MARTINI, HE ORDERS A CUP OF COFFEE. SHORTLY AFTER, THE WAITRESS COMES BACK WITH THE DRINKS. SHE SAYS:
"I'M CONFUSED, WHICH IS WHICH?"
THE LADY SAYS: "I'M THE MARTINI."
THE GENTLEMAN SAYS: "I'M THE COFFEE."
THE WAITRESS PUTS THE DRINKS DOWN AND LEAVES.

SHE IS THE GIN-COLD, INTOXICATING, GIVES YOU A RUSH, MAKES YOU WARM INSIDE, MAKES
YOU LOSE YOUR HEAD; TAKE TOO MUCH, IT MAKES YOU SICK AND SHUTS YOU DOWN.

HE IS THE COFFEE, HOT, STEAMING, FILTERED,
YOU HAVE TO ADD STUFF TO IT TO MAKE IT TASTE GOOD. GRINDS YOUR STOMACH, MAKES
YOU JITTERY, WIRED AND TENSE, BAD TRIP, KEEPS YOU UP, BURNS YOU OUT.

COFFEE AND GIN DON'T MIX, NEVER DO, EVERYBODY KEEPS TRYING AND TRYING TO MAKE IT TASTE GOOD.

. . .

THE SKIES TURNED GREY. THEY CAME BY THE MILLIONS. LOCUSTS. THEY TURNED THE SKY BLACK. THE TOWN TREMBLED. WHAT COULD THEY DO? YOU COULD NOT TRY TO REASON WITH THEM, YOU COULDN'T ARREST THEM (YOU WOULD GO HOARSE READING THEM THEIR RIGHTS) THE

**LOCUSTS WERE DEVOURING ALL PLANT LIFE, BREEDING, BECOMING STRONGER. THERE WAS ONLY ONE THING THAT COULD BE DONE. THE PEOPLE HEARD IT ON THE RADIO: KILL THEM, DESTROY THEM, INCINERATE THEM. KILL, DESTROY, INCINERATE. IT SOUNDED LIKE A WAR. THE LOCUSTS CAME AND RAVAGED THE TOWN. WITHOUT HATRED, WITHOUT JUDGEMENT. THE PEOPLE WERE TOLD TO KILL, THEY KILLED, THEY DESTROYED, THEY INCINERATED. THEY HATED THE INSECTS THAT HAD OVERRUN THEM. THEY SCREAMED AND LASHED OUT AT THEM. THE BUGS HAD NO BRAINS. THEY WERE FAR BELOW THE PEOPLE, YET THEY INSPIRED FEAR, HATRED AND DISSENSION AMONGST THEM. THE PEOPLE SAW AN ENEMY WHERE THERE WASN'T ONE. INSECTS TURNED HUMANS INTO IRRATIONAL IDIOTS, AND I THOUGHT THIS WAS COOL.**

. . .

**DON'T GET ALL UPTIGHT. RELAX, REALLY, YOU COULD PULL A MUSCLE OR SOMETHING. YOU CUT THEM, THEY BLEED.**

YOU SHOOT THEM, YOU BEAT THEM, THEY DIE. IT'S SIMPLE. IT'S JUST FLESH IN YOUR HANDS. IT'S JUST BODIES LYING AT YOUR FEET. IT'S OK TO WANT TO "DO IT." IT'S NOT BAD TO "DO IT." IT'S OK TO MOW THEM DOWN, IT'S OK TO KILL THEM. THAT'S WHAT THEY ARE THERE FOR, NOW THERE'S SOME THINGS YOU REALLY SHOULDN'T DO, LIKE GET ALL UPTIGHT AND SHIT, REALLY. KILL, RELAX AND DESTROY. -- AND DON'T SWEAT IT!
. . .

IN THE GINN'S BACKYARD
SHIRTS HANG FROM BRANCHES OF A TREE
THEY LOOK LIKE GHOSTS
BILLOWING SOULS
AT ATTENTION
PETTIBON'S POT PLANT GROWS IN A CLAY POT
HE DOESN'T SMOKE POT
HE THINKS IT'S FUNNY
MS. GINN SITS IN A LAWN CHAIR
READING A BOOK
ABOUT ADOLF HITLER
I SIT IN THE SHED

**LISTEN TO THE MC5
AND WRITE THIS.**
. . .


**I SAW GOD
WHILE I WAS FUCKING YOUR MOTHER
I SAW GOD
WHILE I WAS MAKING YOUR WIFE SUCK MY
COCK
I SAW GOD WHILE I WAS KILLING YOUR KIDS
I SAW GOD IN THE LUCKY MARKET
DIRTY - GREASY
KILLER
KILLER
LOVER
LOVER
GOD SMILES DOWN ON ME
HE MAKES THE SUN SHINE
FOR ME
I'VE SEEN GOD
YOU HAVEN'T
I SAW GOD
WHILE I WAS CHOKING YOU
  -- HE WAS SMILING.**
. . .

THIS LADY BLEW HER BRAINS OUT IN A PARKING LOT IN LINCOLN, NEBRASKA. SHE SAT AGAINST A WALL AND BLEW HER BRAINS OUT WITH A SHOTGUN. NO NOTE, NO ATTENTION-GETTING DISPLAY. SHE DIED ALONE. AT NIGHT THE WALL GLOWS WHERE HER BRAINS SPLATTERED. I WONDER IF THIS WILL BECOME THE PLACE TO "DO IT." PEOPLE WILL COME TO THE SPOT AND BLOW THEIR SKULLS APART. AT NIGHT THE WALL GLOWS WHERE HER BRAINS SPLATTERED.

. . .

YOU KNOW WHAT THEY SAY:
A MAN'S GOT TO DO WHAT
A BRAINLESS IDIOT'S GOT TO DO.

. . .

GOT A SHIELD OF ARMOR
WRAPPED TIGHT AROUND MY SOUL
SO TIGHT, SOMETIMES I CAN'T
EVEN GET IN OR OUT. HELD PRISONER
TO MYSELF BY MYSELF.

. . .

I HAD A DINNER PARTY. I SERVED MY GUESTS MY FATHER'S HEAD IN A WONDERFUL MUSTARD SAUCE, THEY LOVED IT. EVERYBODY EATS WHEN THEY COME TO MY HOUSE.
. . .

OH BABY
YOU GOTTA BE GOOD TO YOUR MAN
HE WORKS SO HARD FOR YOU BABY
HE WANTS TO BE A GOOD DOG FOR YOU BABY
HE WANTS TO CALL YOU BABY, MOMMA
YOU GOTTA PLEASE YOUR MAN
TAKE HIM BY THE HAND
LOOK INTO HIS EYES
TAKE HIM INTO THE BEDROOM
LAY HIM DOWN
LAY HIM DOWN
TURN OFF THE LIGHTS
MAKE HIM FEEL GOOD
MAKE HIM FEEL GOOD
YOU KNOW HOW
USE YOUR MOUTH
MAKE HIM FEEL GOOD
LISTEN TO HIS BREATHING

**IN**
**OUT**
**IN**
**OUT**
**YEA, HE'S BREATHING HARD**
**HE'S CALLING YOU BABY**
**REACH UNDER THE PILLOW**
**PULL OUT THE KNIFE**
**CUT**
**IT**
**OFF**
**THE WHOLE THING**
**CUT IT OFF**
**LISTEN TO HIM SCREAM**
**LISTEN TO HIM SCREAM**
**GO TO THE KITCHEN**
**WASH YOUR MOUTH OUT**
**MEN ARE PIGS**
**YES**
**MEN ARE PIGS**
**TAKE HIS COCK**
**PUT IT IN AN ENVELOPE**
**SEND IT TO ME**
**DO IT**
**TONIGHT**
**CUT IT OFF**

**RIP IT OUT**
**MEN ARE PIGS**
**SEND IT TO ME**
**NO ONE UNDERSTANDS YOU**
**LIKE I DO**
. . .

**HE BOUGHT THE STUFF FROM A GUY IN A BEAT-UP PINTO. HE WENT HOME. HE FIXED. HE TIED OFF. SUNK THE NAIL INTO HIS ARM. THE SUN CAME STREAMING IN THRU THE WINDOW. GOD WAS BORN.**
. . .

**MADONNA -- SHE MAKES ME WANT TO DRINK BEER, SHE MAKES ME WANT TO DRIVE FAST AND GO BOWLING, SHE MAKES ME WANT TO SHOP AT SEARS, SHE MAKES ME WANT TO KICK VEGETARIANS WHEN I HEAR HER SING, I KNOW SHE'S SINGING TO ME, SHE WANTS TO GET NASTY WITH ME.**
**WHEN I SEE HER FACE**
**WHEN I SEE HER EYES**
**WHEN I SEE HER LIPS**
**TALKING TO ME**
**TELLING ME TO COME ON,**

**I GET TO FEELING MEAN
I GET TO FEELING LIKE
I WANNA DO A WHOLE
LOT OF PUSHUPS
OR GO TO A HARD-
WARE STORE. THEN
I HAVE TO COOL DOWN
I GOTTA COOL DOWN
IT'S EITHER GONNA BE:
A COLD SHOWER,
OR A BRUCE SPRINGSTEEN RECORD.
. . .**

**SAW YOU WALKING DOWN
THE TRAIL
SINGING A DEAD BLACK BIRD SONG
GETTING SMALL IN
THE EYES, NEEDLE
HANGING OUT OF YOUR ARM
TALKING ABOUT THE
DIVINE PUNISHMENT
AND SCREAMING
AT THE GODS
AND HOW YOU GOTTA
GET OUT OF HERE AND HOW
IT'S SUCH A SHAME TO HAVE TO**

## GO SO SOON.
. . .

I like taking my dog for a walk. He really is man's best friend. I have a collar around his neck. I have him on a leash. The leather feels good in my hand. I dig ownership. I've got a wife and a dog. I can kick them and they always come back to me, to be forgiven by me. I like the dog better, he depends on me, if I don't feed him, he doesn't eat. I like jerking his leash and watching him choke. He does not even look up, he just makes harsh rasping sounds with his throat. I say "sit!" to the dog. The dog sits. Sometimes I make him sit and I just stare at him. The dog gets nervous, he gets an upset look in his eyes, he looks away and then back again. His body starts to shake and tremble. He wants to get up to come over to me and lie at my feet. I walk over to him, I raise my hand over his head and hold it there for a minute or two. The dog is shaking and making a low whining sound, finally I pat him on the head and say "Howza abouta walk!" and I clap my hands. The dog gets up and is so happy that I'm not mad that he starts to bark.

He is a happy dog. He does not question me.
I snap my fingers and he brings me his leash.
I own him. He brings his leash to me doesn't
he?
. . .

STANDING ON THE ROOF
JUST AFTER THE RAIN FELL
OZONE
SIRENS
STARING OUT
FEEL LIKE JUMPING OFF?
ALL THE TIME, YES.
MOIST BREEZE
2:47 AM
MAYBE THE SUN WON'T COME UP TODAY
MAYBE IF THAT HAPPENS,
ALL THE BUS DRIVERS WOULD BE
MORE POLITE
THE CABBIES WOULDN'T BE INSANE
AND THIS NICE STILLNESS WOULD LAST
AWHILE
BUT
THE SUN IS ON ITS WAY
AND I'M NOT GOING TO LET IT
BURN ME UP TODAY

IF I COULD FLY OFF THIS ROOF
RIGHT NOW
I WOULD
BUT IF I FALL DOWN AGAIN
I DON'T THINK I'LL BE ABLE TO HANDLE IT
SO I'LL JUST STAY ALIVE
AMONGST THE ANIMALS
OF THE SUMMER

. . .

I WAS AT THIS GUY'S HOUSE. I MET THIS GIRL WHO WAS HANGING OUT THERE. SHE WAS REAL PRETTY, SHE HAD BROWN EYES AND DARK HAIR. SHE WAS SOFT-SPOKEN AND REAL NICE. I KNOW THAT EVERYONE HAS THEIR OWN LIFE AND THEY CAN DO WHAT THEY WANT AND YOU SHOULDN'T THINK ANYTHING OF IT OR ANYTHING, BUT MAN, I COULD NOT HELP BUT FLINCH A LITTLE WHEN I SAW ALL THOSE NEEDLE MARKS ON HER ARMS, THEY LOOKED SO SORE. HATEFUL LITTLE HOLES. I WANTED TO SAY SOMETHING, BUT I DID NOT.

. . .

I HAVE COLORS ON MY BACK

**I AM MARKED
BRANDED
CHOSEN
THE AIR TEARS AT ME
SOMETIMES I FEEL
LIKE THE GAS CHAMBERS
AND THE OVENS
OF THE WORLD
ARE INSIDE ME
READY
TO CHOKE
AND INCINERATE
EVERYTHING
THAT WOUNDS MY EYES.
AND SOMETIMES
I THINK
THAT EVERYTHING
AND EVERYONE
WOUNDS MY EYES
AND THE PAIN
BRINGS A LUCIDITY
THAT MAKES SENSE
OF THE IDEA OF
HEALING THE WOUNDS
AND BRINGS THE STREETS
TO A BOIL**

. . .

**WHEN I LOOK INTO HER EYES
I SEE
A FIRE BURNING
NOT THE FIRE OF DESIRE
NOT THE FIRE OF LOVE
THE FIRE OF DEAD BODIES
PILED IN MOUNDS
THE FIRE OF PLAGUE & PESTILENCE
SHE IS NAPALM
BURNED TO DEATH BY NAPALM
HAVE YOU SEEN THEM RUNNING,
SCREAMING,
FLESH BURNING, CURLING BACK
MY LOVE FOR HER
IS A CRAWLING FAMINE
CLAWING AT HER SOUL
SHE BURNS WITH NAPALM
I CRAVE HER DESTRUCTION
SHE LIGHTS UP THE JUNGLE
SHE BURNS
WITH NAPALM**

. . .

**I'M COMING OUT OF 7-11**

A CAR PULLS UP
THE DOOR OPENS
A MAN YELLS
"OK, FUCK, YOU GO GET THE BEER, I DON'T
CARE!
A PRETTY GIRL GETS OUT
SHE PASSES ME, AND SMILES
HER PERFUME MIXES WITH THE SMELL
OF THE ALCOHOL
ALREADY CONSUMED.
THE MAN IN THE FRONT SEAT
WINKS AT ME
AND WAITS FOR
THE BUD
AND THE BROAD.

. . .

DON'T THINK
DRINK
YES
DRINK YOUR FILL
DRIVE
KILL
YES
IT'S OK, REALLY
IT'S OK TO MOW DOWN

INNOCENT PEOPLE?
YES
WHY?
BECAUSE NO ONE IS INNOCENT
OR SOME SHIT
IT'S A GOOD RAP
WHEN YOU GET
DRUNK
WHEN YOU GET
BEHIND THE WHEEL
WHEN YOU GET
PULLED OVER
FOR WIPING OUT
SOME PEOPLE
WHO GOT
IN YOUR WAY
. . .

I DON'T WANT TO GET OUT OF BED TODAY.

I PULL THE COVERS OVER MY HEAD. I START TO GNAW AT THE FLESH ON MY CHEST. I RIP PIECES OF MY SKIN AWAY FROM MY BODY. I SWALLOW HUNKS OF MY FLESH. I CHEW A LARGE HOLE IN MY CHEST. THERE. FINE. I CRAWL INTO THE

HOLE. I REACH MY HAND OUT THE BLEEDING FLESH HOLE AND PULL THE COVERS OVER THE CORPSE'S FACE. THERE. FINE. DARK, WARM, QUIET. I TAKE OUT THE GUN. I PUT THE BARREL IN MY MOUTH. I PULL THE TRIGGER. MY BRAINS SPLATTER ALL OVER MY RIB CAGE. I DIED INSIDE MYSELF. GOODBYE. THERE. FINE.

. . .

MAN AND WOMAN
FOREVER RUPTURED
FOREVER SEVERED
CLUTCHING
CLAWING
EACH OTHER'S FLESH
FUCKING IN SHALLOW GRAVES
ROLLING IN BLOOD SOAKED DIRT
HE LOOKS INTO HER EYES
HE REACHES INSIDE HER
DEEP INSIDE HER
HE RIPS HER UTERUS OUT
AND SHAKES IT IN HER FACE.
HE SCREAMS "WHO'S IDEA
WAS THIS?"

. . .

I DRILLED A HOLE INTO THE BACK OF MY HEAD. IT WAS EASY. I TOOK A BLACK AND DECKER POWER DRILL AND PUT IT TO MY HEAD. THE DRILL BIT CHEWED THRU MY SCALP, NO PROBLEM, A LITTLE BIT OF SMOKE CAME UP WHEN THE BIT HIT MY SKULL. I GAVE IT A GOOD PUSH AND IT CRUNCHED THRU TO MY BRAIN. I STUFFED A BIT OF PAPER TOWEL IN THE HOLE, NOW, WHEN THE PRESSURE GETS TO BE TOO MUCH, I PULL OUT THE CORK AND LET MY BRAINS DRAIN OUT SOME. A LITTLE BIT OF STICKY JUICE COMES OUT. THE PRESSURE'S OFF. IF YOU WANT TO GET RID OF PROBLEMS, GET RID OF THEM.

. . .

A GUY GOES INTO A LIQUOR STORE, HE ROBS THE PLACE. WHILST ROBBING THE STORE, HE SHOOTS AND KILLS A MAN. FINE. HE IS APPREHENDED AND TRIED. HE IS FOUND GUILTY OF 1ST DEGREE MURDER AND SENTENCED TO DIE. FINE. HE IS TAKEN TO THE ELECTRIC CHAIR. HE IS STRAPPED IN AND GIVEN HIS LAST RITES. A

**MAN GOES TO THE CONTROL ROOM AND PULLS THE SWITCH, THE MAN IN THE CHAIR DIES, FINE. NOW, THAT GUY WHO PULLED THE SWITCH IS A KILLER, YES. OK, HE GOES TO COURT, PLEADS GUILTY TO 1ST DEGREE MURDER. HE IS SENTENCED TO DIE IN THE ELECTRIC CHAIR, HE IS STRAPPED IN AND READ HIS RITES. A MAN PULLS THE SWITCH AND KILLS THE KILLER WHO KILLED THE KILLER, THE MAN IS TAKEN TO COURT AND ... YOU GET THE PICTURE.**
**. . .**

**I SAW THIS MOVIE ON TV TODAY. THIS POLISH SPY WAS IMPERSONATING ADOLF HITLER. HE WAS ON A FLIGHT WITH A BUNCH OF OTHER POLES DRESSED IN NAZI UNIFORMS. THE ONLY GERMANS ON THE PLANE WERE THE TWO PILOTS. TO GET RID OF THEM, A SOLDIER CAME TO THE COCKPIT AND TOLD THE PILOTS THAT THE FUHRER WANTED TO SPEAK TO THEM PERSONALLY TO COMPLIMENT THEM ON THEIR SKILL. THE TWO PILOTS RAN DOWN THE AISLE TO MEET THE MAN. THE HITLER IMPERSONATOR OPENED UP THE SIDE DOOR**

AND SAID "JUMP." THEY DID, BOTH OF THEM, THEY SALUTED AND JUMPED OUT, THEY DID NOT QUESTION THEIR LEADER. WHAT CONTROL, WHAT CHARISMA. SOMETIMES I WISH I COULD LOAD EVERYONE IN THE WORLD IN A PLANE AND TELL THEM TO JUMP.

. . .

TOO SICK AND FREAKED OUT TO MASTURBATE, TOO SICK AND FREAKED OUT TO LAUGH AT HITLER (I NOW LAUGH WITH HIM). TOO SICK AND FREAKED OUT NOT TO WANT A BULLET FOR EVERY PASSERBY, TOO SICK AND FREAKED OUT TO BREATHE, TOO SICK AND FREAKED OUT TO CARE, TOO SICK AND FREAKED OUT TO THINK OF ANYTHING BUT THE ANNIHILATION OF MY MIND AND DENIAL OF MY LIFE. SO SICK AND FREAKED OUT THAT I THINK EVERYONE IS MY FRIEND. TOO SICK AND FREAKED OUT.

. . .

I WAS DRIVING DOWN SANTA MONICA BLVD. I PASSED LA CIENEGA BLVD., PAST THE HOTEL WHERE JIM MORRISON USED TO

CAMP OUT IN, THE SAME HOTEL THAT JANIS JOPLIN DIED IN, I PASSED THAT. I DROVE BY THE HOTEL TROPICANA, I SAW A SLIM YOUNG MAN NAILED TO A WOODEN CROSS, INSTEAD OF NAILS, HE HAD SYRINGES POUNDED THRU HIS PALMS AND FEET. HIS UPWARD GAZE WAS BRILLIANT AND INTENSE. SOME MANAGER-TYPE LADY WAS TALKING TO SOME MEN THAT WERE STATIONED AT HIS FEET, TELLING THEM TO LOAD THE SAINT IN THE CAR, HE HAD TO GO DO AN APPEARANCE AT A RECORD STORE, I DROVE ON, SURE THAT I HAD SEEN THE REAL THING.

. . .

BE MY OASIS, MAKE ME WANT TO STAY BY LETTING ME GO AWAY WHEN I NEED TO GO AWAY. BE MY FOREST, MAKE ME WANT TO STAY BY UNDERSTANDING MY NEED TO WALK ALONE IN THE DESERT. BE MY SUNSHINE, MAKE ME WANT TO STAY BY KNOWING HOW GOOD IT IS TO RUN IN MOON LIT FIELDS.

. . .

**THIS MORNING THEY FOUND YOU, IN AN ALLEY, DEAD, FACE DOWN, ALL SHOT UP. YOUR BULLET-RIDDEN BLACK-AND-WHITE STILL RUNNING, THE LADY ON THE 11:00 NEWS SAID THAT YOUR FELLOW OFFICERS ARE STILL LOOKING FOR A REASON WHY SOMEONE KILLED YOU. -- I DID IT BECAUSE YOU ARE A FUCKING COP, YOU ARE A PIG, AND I AM A PIG KILLER.**

**. . .**

**AGE 19**
**CORBEL LABS**
**ECTROMELIA**
**GAS**
**MICE LEAPING UP**
**SIMULTANEOUSLY**
**RELEASING SHIT/PISS**
**DIED WITH EYES OPEN**
**LYING IN A POOL OF**
**URINE**
**50 HOURS OF KILLING**
**BOXES OF DEAD**
**TAKEN TO THE N.I.H.**
**FACILITY**
**SOME WERE DUMPED**

IN A DUMPSTER AT 7-11
SOME WERE DUMPED
IN A DUMPSTER AT BURGER KING
LOTS OF DEATH
DEAD BODIES
POISON GAS
. . .

MY LOVE RUNS DEEPER THAN THE WOUNDS I INFLICT UPON MYSELF, DEEPER THAN THE SWEAT THAT POURS FROM MY BODY, MY LOVE RUNS DEEPER THAN THE TEARS THAT ROLL DOWN MY FACE.

MY HATE RUNS DEEPER THAN THE WOUNDS I INFLICT UPON MYSELF DEEPER THAN THE SWEAT THAT POURS FROM MY BODY, MY HATE RUNS DEEPER THAN THE TEARS THAT ROLL DOWN MY FACE.
. . .

COCKROACHES ARE YOUR GODS. YOU ARE WEAK. YOU SHOULD PRAY TO THEM. THEY ARE A MORE PERFECT LIFE FORM THAN YOU. YOU ARE FUCKED UP, WITH YOUR IDIOTIC IDIOSYNCRASIES. YOU HAVE

ANALYSTS, TRANQUILIZERS, YOU NEED VACATIONS, YOU START WARS, YOU COMMIT SUICIDE, YOU STEAL, YOU LIE, YOU CHEAT. YOU ARE WEAK. YOU CANNOT SURVIVE, YOU ARE TOO BUSY HAULING AROUND THAT BIG BRAIN OF YOURS, YOU HAVE TO BUILD JAILS TO KEEP YOUR KIND FROM KILLING YOU! YOU KILL EVERYTHING. YOU LIVE IN FEAR. YOU COULD NEVER LIVE WITH THE SIMPLICITY AND BEAUTY OF THE ROACH. YOU HAVE ABORTIONS. YOU ENGAGE IN MEANINGLESS ACTIVITY. YOU ARE WEAK, COCKROACHES ARE YOUR GODS. YOU ARE NOT EVEN FIT TO KISS THE SMOOTH BELLY SCALES OF THE MOTHER ROACH, YOU ARE REPULSED BY THEM, YOU FEAR THEM. THERE ARE MORE OF THEM THAN THERE ARE OF YOU, YOU GET SQUEAMISH AT JUST THE SIGHT, THEY MAKE YOU SICK. YOU ARE WEAK. COCKROACHES ARE YOUR GODS, GIVE UP YOUR PLATE OF FOOD TO THEM, WHETHER YOU DO OR NOT, THEY WILL SURVIVE YOU AND YOUR STUPIDITY. YOU TRY TO KILL THEM WITH GAS AND POISON JUST LIKE YOU DO TO YOUR OWN KIND, THE ROACH COMES BACK, STRONGER, FASTER,

MORE IMMUNE. YOU WATCH TELEVISION, YOU LOCK YOUR DOORS TO PROTECT YOURSELF FROM YOUR RACE. YOU PUT NEEDLES IN YOUR ARMS, YOU SELL YOUR BODIES, YOU FIND NEW AND INVENTIVE WAYS TO MUTILATE YOURSELVES AND OTHERS. YOU ARE WEAK. COCKROACHES ARE YOUR GODS.

. . .

I DON'T HAVE TINY PAIN, SORRY, FRESH OUT, I HAVE BIGGER, NEW AND IMPROVED PAIN, GOOD PAIN. PAIN OF THE HIGHEST QUALITY TO BE SURE. AND I WEAR IT LIKE A $200 SUIT.

. . .

I GOT A BRAIN
BUT I DON'T KNOW IT
I GOT FEELING
BUT I DON'T SHOW IT

ALL MY FRIENDS
ARE GOING NOWHERE
THEY ARE NOBODYS
HOW COME I AM ALWAYS
WITH THEM AT THE BAR?

I DRINK TO SINK
PARTYING TAKES AWAY THE PAIN.
I DON'T WANT TO THINK
IF I'M WRECKED THEN I DON'T HAVE TO EXPLAIN

ALL MY BUDDIES
GIVE ME THE PUSH
I FLY THE FLAG
OF ANHEUSER-BUSCH

WHEN I'M WASTED I KNOW THAT
I HAVE ESCAPED THE GRIND, OF 9 TO 5
BUT SOMETIMES I THINK THAT I'M
RUNNING FROM SOMETHING.

I HEARD ON THE RADIO THAT EVERY-
BODY'S WORKING FOR THE WEEKEND.
WHEN DOES THE WEEKEND START?
WHAT COMES AT THE END OF THE WEEK?
THE END?

PICTURE A TIRED DOG CHASING ITS
TAIL.

. . .

**WHEN YOU FINALLY HIT THE BOTTOM, NO REALLY, THE BOTTOM, WHERE YOU CANNOT POSSIBLY GO LOWER, THERE IS A GUY TRYING TO SELL YOU THE BROOKLYN BRIDGE OR A ONE WAY BUS TICKET TO PHILADELPHIA, DON'T SAY I DIDN'T WARN YOU.**

. . .

**ATTENTION! ATTENTION! HUSBANDS AND WIVES WITH YOUNG, OR THOSE EXPECTING YOUNG ONES! IN THE NEAR FUTURE...YOU WILL BE RELOCATED! YOU WILL BE STATIONED AT BREEDING CENTERS. THE MALES WILL BE SLAUGHTERED PAINLESSLY. THE FEMALES WILL BE KEPT IN LARGE PENS, ONE MALE TO STUD PENS OF 30 BREEDERS -- YOU BREEDERS WILL HAVE A MEANINGFUL AND PRODUCTIVE LIFE. YOU WILL HAVE A CHILD EVERY 11 MONTHS UNTIL YOU ARE NO LONGER ADEQUATE FOR BREEDING STATUS. THEN YOU WILL BE PUT TO SLEEP -- PAINLESSLY. IN PLAIN WORDS: YOU WILL NO LONGER BE ALLOWED TO HAVE CHILDREN UNLESS THEY ARE KEPT**

AND MAINTAINED IN DESIGNATED BREEDING CENTERS. IF ANY INFANTS OR YOUNG ARE FOUND OUTSIDE THE BREEDING CONFINES, THEY WILL BE IMMEDIATELY DESTROYED, ALONG WITH THE "PARENTS" OF COURSE. THANK YOU FOR YOUR COOPERATION.

. . .

THEY ARE ROLLING OUT THE CARPET FOR YOU TO GET SICK ON. THEY ARE GETTING YOUR HEAD SIZE FOR A CUSTOM FITTED LAMPSHADE. THEY ARE LIGHTING 23 CANDLES TONIGHT. 23 LITTLE FLAMES FOR YOU TO BLOW OUT. 23 YEARS IN ONE BREATH. I AM IN THE BACKGROUND - YARD DIGGING A HOLE, WAITING; FOR THE PARTY TO BE OVER. MAKE A WISH.

. . .

FAMILY MAN, WITH YOUR GLANCES MY WAY
TAKING NO CHANCES ON THE NEW DAY
FAMILY MAN, WITH YOUR LIFE ALL PLANNED
YOUR SANDCASTLE BUILT
SMILING THRU YOUR GUILT
HERE I COME
HERE I COME FAMILY MAN

I COME TO INFECT
I COME TO RAPE YOUR WOMAN
I COME TO TAKE YOUR CHILDREN
INTO THE STREET
I COME FOR YOUR FAMILY MAN
FAMILY MAN, WITH YOUR CHRISTMAS LIGHTS
ALREADY UP, YOU'RE SUCH A MAN WHEN YOU'RE
PUTTING UP YOUR CHRISTMAS LIGHTS, FIRST
ON THE BLOCK. I WANT TO CRUCIFY YOU ON
YOUR FRONT DOOR WITH NAILS FROM YOUR
WELL-STOCKED GARAGE. FAMILY MAN - SAINT
DAD -- FATHER ON FIRE -- I'VE COME TO
INCINERATE -- I'VE COME HOME.
. . .

THE MANIFESTATION MANIFESTS ITSELF IN
EVERY WAY IMAGINABLE. WE ARE FOLDED,
SPINDLED AND MUTILATED. WE ARE NOT
BLINDED! DISILLUSIONMENT SMASHES ITS
FIST THRU THE PAVEMENT AND GRABS US
BY THE ANKLES, TRIPS US UP, TRIPS US
OUT. OUR EYES FILL WITH DIRT, WE TRY TO

SCREAM BUT OUR MOUTHS BECOME FILLED WITH THE DIRT, WE SPIT AND CURSE BUT WE EVENTUALLY CHOMP THE BIT AND PULL FORWARD AND LURCH TO THE NEXT SCREECHING HALT, THE BRAKES, (OUR EYES) KEEP US IN OUR SEATS. WE GO ALONG WITH IT DUE TO A SAFE FACADE OF IGNORANCE BUT WE ARE ALWAYS LOOKING THRU THE KEYHOLE, PROBABLY THE CLOSEST WE SHALL COME TO RECKONING. WE ARE BORN, IMMEDIATELY INFECTED, AND PLAGUED FOR THE REST OF OUR LIVES, OUR PRIVATE ETERNITY, OUR OWN FOREVER. ALL OF OUR THOUGHTS ARE PURELY IMPURE, WE TRY TO UNDERSTAND THE PAIN OF OTHERS BUT WE CAN ONLY UNDERSTAND IT OUR WAY. WE SIT IN YOUR APARTMENT. WE ARE LEECHES, SUCKING EACH OTHER DRY. WE ARE EACH OTHER'S HEROIN, ALWAYS TRYING TO FIX OUR RELATIONSHIP WHICH IS FULL OF HOLES AND SINKING FAST. WANTING TO KICK SO BAD, WE ARE MONKEYS ON A MONKEY'S BACK, I'M A JUNKIE YOU'RE MY MONKEY. THE SUN FALLS LIKE A DYING CREATURE THRU THE BURNING AIR, THE AIR THAT

STINGS OUR EYES, AS THE GASPING FINAL RAYS PASS US, WE TAKE OFF OUR CLOTHES, WE FIND OUR BODIES CLAWED, DEFILED, SCARRED, DISTORTED, MISSHAPEN, MONKEY ON A MONKEY'S BACK, HOLDING ON TO EACH OTHER'S TAIL, WE RUN IN CIRCLES JUST AS FAST AS WE CAN GO. HAVE YOU EVER PRESSED YOUR HANDS AGAINST THE WALL AND THOUGHT, "DAMN, I'M GONNA DIE IN THIS PLACE." WE ARE STUCK HERE. MOORED, ENTRENCHED BY MORTALITY, THE STIFLING STRAIGHT-JACKET OF HUMANITY DOES ITS JOB. WE ARE PASSED AROUND, HAND-TO-HAND AND LED TO THE WHIPPING-POST WHERE OUR LOVERS ARE WAITING. THEY HAND US WHIPS AND WE BEAT OURSELVES INTO SLEEP. WE BEAT OURSELVES TO DEATH. THEY LAY US DOWN, LAY US LOW, WHIP IN ONE HAND, A BLOODY MONKEY'S TAIL IN THE OTHER.

. . .

WE DON'T GIVE BIRTH
WE ABORT, ABORT, ABORT.
JUMP SHIP. DROWNING RATS
WILL CLING WITH A TENACITY

**SELDOM SEEN. I THINK THEY WANT TO LIVE MORE THAN YOU DO, SO WHY DON'T YOU STEP ASIDE.**

**THE EARTH IS INFESTED, CRAWLING WITH LIFE.
LET'S DE-LOUSE IT NOW.**

**HOMICIDE, PATRICIDE, MATRICIDE, GENOCIDE,
DOMESTICIDE.**

. . .

**IN THE DEEP WELL OF THE NIGHT, THE SILENCE SURROUNDS YOU AND SEALS OFF YOUR PORES. A SILENCE SO SILENT AND POWERFUL THAT YOU MIGHT THINK YOU ARE GOING INSANE, YOU HEAR A SONG THAT YOU NEVER HEARD BEFORE, AND YOU THINK THAT YOU ARE GOING INSANE.**

. . .

**THE BABY WAS BORN. A GIRL, SHE HAD HER FATHER'S NOSE AND CHEEKBONES, HER MOTHER'S HIGH FOREHEAD AND EYES,**

**SHE HAD HER FATHER'S KNIFE SCARS AND HER MOTHER'S TRACK MARKS.**

. . .

**LORD,
GIVE ME A GUN
I'LL GIVE YOU ACTS OF SALVATION AND MERCY
GIVE ME A MOBILE ARTILLERY UNIT
I'LL GIVE YOU SOME CONSTRUCTIVE CRITICISM
GIVE ME NAPALM
I'LL TURN THE OTHER CHEEK
GIVE ME A DIME
I'LL CALL IN THE AIR STRIKE
GIVE ME A CHANCE
AND I'LL STOP HUNGER
I'LL STOP DISEASE
I'LL STOP WORLD SUFFERING
GIVE ME A BUTTON
I'LL GIVE YOU PEACE**

. . .

**I'M IN THE KITCHEN, PICKING MEAT OFF THE BONES OF A ROAST CHICKEN I FOUND IN THE OVEN. SOUNDS NICE DOESN'T IT. YES**

**THE CORPSE IS IN A PAN WITH ITS OWN "JUICES." I AM EATING FLESH OFF THE CORPSE'S BONES. IT JUST CAME OUT OF THE OVEN. WHAT'S THE DIFFERENCE BETWEEN "THE OVEN" AND "THE OVENS" AT AUSCHWITZ. THE FLESH IS BURNT TO A CRISP. THE "CHITLINS" ARE BLACK AND COMPACTED LYING AT THE BOTTOM OF THE CHEST CAVITY. "CHITLINS" ARE GOOD IN GRAVY AREN'T THEY WHAT'S THE DIFFERENCE BETWEEN THE CHICKEN'S LIVER AND THE ONE IN THE LITTLE GIRL NEXT DOOR? I AM A VULTURE, PICKING DEAD FLESH OFF THE BONES OF A CORPSE. I RIP A LEG OFF AND SINK MY TEETH IN, MUSCLE, SKIN AND TENDON COME AWAY IN MY MOUTH. THIS IS A "DRUMSTICK"; WE ALL LIKE "DRUMSTICKS." WHY CAN'T I RIP THE LEG OFF THAT LITTLE RED-HAIRED BOY ACROSS THE STREET AND SINK MY TEETH INTO IT? WHAT'S THE PROBLEM? I COOK DEAD BODIES IN MY HOUSE AND THEN I EAT THEM! I LIKE IT!**

**. . .**

I WOULD LIKE TO OPEN A RESTAURANT IN THE SPIRIT OF THOSE TEXAS STEAK HOUSES I HAVE BEEN TO. YOU WALK IN AND PICK OUT THE PIECE OF MEAT YOU WANT AND THE CHEF'S WILL COOK IT FOR YOU ANY WAY YOU PLEASE. IN MY PLACE, I WOULD SERVE HUMAN FLESH. YOU PICK OUT WHAT YOU WANT, THE BODIES WILL BE DISPLAYED ON LARGE HOOKS, YOU CAN HAVE YOUR PICK OF WHAT YOU WANT, BLACK, WHITE, MALE, FEMALE, WHATEVER THE FUCK YOU'LL WANT, I'LL HAVE IT FOR YOU. YOU WANT TO REALLY EAT 13-YEAR-OLD GIRL'S PUSSY? WELL DO IT! WITH SOME SALT, A-1 SAUCE AND A COORS LIGHT TO WASH IT DOWN. HELL, I'LL LET YOU COME BACK AND CUT IT OUT YOURSELF! THAT MOTHERFUCKER WHO RAPED YOUR WIFE AND DAUGHTER AND THEN BLEW HIS BRAINS OUT IN THE LIVING ROOM? BRING DOWN AN ARM OR FLANK, I'LL COOK IT UP FOR YOU. WE'LL SHISHKEBOB HIS PECKER WITH PINEAPPLE AND MUSHROOMS! COME ON DOWN TO HANK'S HOUSE OF FLESH, WHERE YOU ARE WHAT YOU EAT!

. . .

**I HAVE FOUND A
WAY TO BEAT MYSELF.
I WIN BY LOSING, OR
SOMETHING LIKE THAT
. . .**

**I AM TOLD THAT I'M STUPID
SO OK, I'LL BE STUPID
IF I CAN'T REGISTER THE PAIN
THEN IT'S NOT THERE
I'M NOT SO STUPID AFTER ALL.
I'LL SHOW THEM
I HAVE WON
. . .**

**How lame it is for me to sit in some cushy living room watching Apocalypse Now, on video cassette no less. You think you have pain? That guy went up the river to kill a guy. I'm sitting in a suburban living room on a plush carpet with search and destroy tattooed on my back and I'm watching the real thing, it makes touring seem rather easy in comparison. I love that movie. I feel small when I see it because I want to do stuff that is as ultimate. Music is**

a far cry from missions into classified Cambodia. The guy sat in his room in Saigon and was going crazy waiting for a chance to get back to the jungle, and all I do is pull up to a club set up and play for an hour or so, and leave, this is not living and dying, or anything close. I'm sitting in a living room in suburban Seattle with a full stomach, a cup of coffee in my hand, a pillow for my head, shit! That is the case. This nullifies any of my little hardships, I do not know the meaning of grueling. Pain, Pain? Fuck my pain! The muscle aches, the neckaches, so what. I do not know the meaning of pain. "Doesn't your tour schedule tire you out?" I'm still alive aren't I, we can't be pressed that hard. You can't call in an air strike at the Perkins Palace. There is no backstage in the jungle, no soundcheck, no set list, no men's room. What kind of an asshole am I anyway? Sitting on this rug, safe, about to take a hot shower, knowing that when the movie is over, one can flip a switch and watch MTV.

. . .

I SWEAR, THIS MAN CAME IN ONE SIDE OF TOWN RIDIN' BARE ASS BLIND BUCK ASS NAKED ON A THREE LEGGED MULE, WENT OUT THE OTHER SIDE IN A CADILLAC CAR. I DON'T KNOW WHAT WENT ON IN THE MIDDLE, BUT IT MUST HAVE BEEN GOOD.

. . .

DUDE, LIKE I WORK AT THIS MACHINE SHOP. IT SUCKS. I WORK THERE ALL WEEK. WHEN FRIDAY COMES, I BUST LOOSE. I PARTY THE FUCK DOWN! ME AND MY FRIENDS CALL THE WEEKEND "THE 'END" FOR SHORT. WE SAY STUFF LIKE "TWO MORE DAYS 'TILL THE 'END." SOUNDS COOL. THE 'END IS COMING DUDE DON'T SAY I DIDN'T WARN YA! SOMETIMES THE 'END STARTS THURSDAY AT LUNCH. DUDE, THE 'END IS ALWAYS NEAR SO GRAB A SIX, A BROAD AND PARTY!

. . .

I SAW A COLOR PICTURE OF A BLACK MAN HANGING BY HIS NECK. THE PICTURE WAS NOT OLD. HE WAS DRESSED LIKE YOU OR I MIGHT DRESS. IT WAS SAID TO BE K.K.K. KILLING. THERE WAS THIS BLACK DUDE

SWINGING FROM A ROPE THAT WAS TIED TO A TREE BRANCH. I BELIEVE IN WHEELS, LIKE WHAT GOES AROUND COMES AROUND AND ALL THAT. I WONDER WHAT THE HANGPERSON OR HANGPERSONS HEAR AT NIGHT. THAT IS A MIGHTY WHEEL, A CRUSHING WHEEL. I WONDER IF THE HANGPERSON OR HANGPERSONS EVER HEAR THE ROAR OF THEIR WHEEL, ROLLING DOWN THE TRAIL. I AM TALKING ABOUT THE ROAR OF THE WHEEL.

. . .

I WAS WALKING DOWN A STREET DOWN IN NEW ORLEANS. I WAS WALKING PAST A GRAVEYARD. THE DEAD WERE ALL ABOVE GROUND IN STONE MAUSOLEUMS. THIS DUDE COMES UP TO ME AND ASKS ME FOR HELP. HE SAYS: "I'M DEAD! I KEEP TRYING TO ENTER MY MAUSOLEUM AND I KEEP GETTING SPAT OUT! LOOTERS CAME AND TOOK ALL MY CLOTHES!" I WAS ABOUT TO SAY, I MEAN THIS GUY RUNNING AROUND IN BOXER SHORTS? "LOOK I'M TRYING TO BE A GOOD CORPSE, DECOMPOSING, WORMS THE WHOLE BIT BUT NOTHING'S HAPPENING,

I'VE BEEN HERE A WEEK AND A HALF!" I ASKED HIM IF HE WAS SURE HE WAS DEAD. HE SAID "YES I'M SURE! LOOK!" HE HANDED ME HIS DEATH CERTIFICATE, HE WAS DEAD ALL RIGHT. YOU KNOW WHAT THEY SAY, YOU CAN'T KEEP A GOOD MAN DOWN.

. . .

He came home after work, like he did Monday thru Friday. He felt good, he parked the car in the garage and came in thru the kitchen door. His wife was in the kitchen, cooking dinner. She smiles, "Hi honey," she said. She went to the refrigerator and got him a Coors Light. He looked out the window, the front lawn was good, trimmed, green. His wife talked about all kinds of things he didn't care about. That's good, women are suppose to talk about PTA meetings and casseroles. Good. She was ok. The house smelled clean, un-lived in. A real castle. He went into the bathroom to use the toilet. He thought about those magazines he saw at the newsstand. Young girls engaging in oral copulation with young males. That's what he wanted! Yes. He wanted to tell his wife,

"Madge, suck me!" but he thought of her aprons and her casseroles and knew that he could not do it. What if he could! She might do it, then at the end (when he came), she would probably bolt downstairs and wash her mouth out with sink cleanser. He started to get an erection. He thought about masturbating, he hadn't done that since he was in college. He started to cry. Yes cry. Tears splashed onto his bare legs. The stench of his own waste filled his nostrils. He felt clean, unlived in, held prisoner by the life he created for himself. His life was driveways, casseroles, television, miles of front lawns, kids and then death. Dinner would be ready soon.

. . .

THE WHITES STOOD, SHACKLED AND BOUND. THEY LINED THE STREETS OF HOLLYWOOD. SOME WERE BEING LOADED INTO BUSES, OTHERS WERE BEING AUCTIONED OFF RIGHT THERE AT HOLLYWOOD AND VINE. A FATHER STOOD TREMBLING AND CRYING SILENTLY AS HE WATCHED HIS DAUGHTER BEING HAGGLED OVER BY BLACK MEN. SHE STOOD ON A KNUDSON'S ORANGE CRATE

NAKED. MEN WERE LAUGHING, GRABBING HER BREASTS AND FINGERING HER AND SAMPLING THE GOODS IN GENERAL. A MAN WITH A LARGE ERECTION WAS THE HIGHEST BIDDER. HE GRABBED HER ROUGHLY AND LED HER AWAY. THE TWO GOT ON AN R.T.D BUS AND WERE GONE.

. . .

YOU'RE WALKING
DOWN A STREET
A STREET ALL BY YOUR
SELF. YOU SEE A
CAR IN THE DISTANCE.
THE CAR PULLS UP
THERE IS A MAN
IN THE CAR, HE'S
CALLING YOU, WAVING
YOU OVER TO THE CAR
DON'T JUST STAND THERE
RUN! --
RIGHT OVER TO HIM --
HE HAS CANDY, YOU
LIKE CANDY, HE'S GOT
IT, YOU WANT IT.
GET THE FUCK IN

THE CAR.
GET
IN
THE
CAR
HE WANTS TO HURT
YOU AND TOUCH YOU AND
GIVE YOU CANDY -- LET HIM
HE WANTS YOUR PANTS DOWN
HE WANTS TO GIVE YOU CANDY
HE IS PULLING YOUR PANTS DOWN
AND STUFFING CANDY INTO YOUR MOUTH
YOU LIKE CANDY -- SO EAT IT!
HE'S PULLING YOUR PANTS DOWN, LET HIM!
HE IS GOING TO RIP AT YOUR PRIVATE
PARTS
WITH A PAIR OF PLIERS.
SO WHAT.
IT'S GOING TO HURT AND KILL YOU,
MUTILATE AND DEFILE YOU.
DEAD CHILD
SHALLOW GRAVE.
AUTUMN LEAVES.
...I LOVE AUTUMN TIME. I CAN REMEMBER
THAT OCTOBER, WALKING WITH THAT GIRL
DOWN WISCONSIN AVENUE. THE SUN WAS

SETTING AND THE AIR WAS CRISP AND YOU COULD SMELL THE SMOKE FROM THE FIRE PLACES. THE LEAVES WERE FALLING FROM THE TREES AND SWIRLING AT OUR FEET. I WANTED THAT NIGHT TO LAST FOREVER I LOVE THE...DON'T BLOW YOUR CHANCE AT ROMANCE, ALWAYS TALK TO STRANGERS, GET IN THE FUCKING CAR.

. . .

WHEN I SEE THE GIRLS WALKING DOWN THE STREET I WANT TO FUCK, I GET TO FEELING CRAZY. I WANT TO BREED, I WANT TO EAT A MILE OF PUSSY. OUT OF MY HEAD.

. . .

I SEE THE GIRLS IN WESTWOOD WALKING WITH THEIR BOY FRIENDS, I WANT TO GET A BIG GUN AND SHOOT. KILL THE BOY FRIENDS. I WANT TO EAT A MILE OF PUSSY. I GET TO WANTING A GUN TO SHOOT, SHOOT, SHOOT. I SEE THEIR LEGS IN SHORT SKIRTS AND AM LED TO BELIEVE THAT I AM SOMETHING DIRTY AND VILE AND I WANT TO SHOOT GUNS. I SEE THE GIRLS

IN MALIBU IN THEIR SKIRTS AND I KNOW I
AM ALIVE MERCILESSLY SO. I'M SO DIRTY
AND VILE AND ALIVE THAT I WANT TO GET A
GUN AND SHOOT EVERY THING THAT MOVES.
. . .

SITTING IN MY APT.
(I LIVE IN AN APT.)
JUNE
STIFLING HOT
I CAME HOME
FROM WORK
THERE IS A GIRL
SLEEPING IN MY BED.
I GO TO THE OTHER ROOM
WHERE MY ROOMMATE IS
I POINT TO MY BED
HE SMILES
AND SHRUGS
I PUT ON A RECORD AND GET A COKE
AND LISTEN TO THE VIETNAMESE CHILDREN
PLAY OUTSIDE
AND WONDER
WHAT AM I SUPPOSED TO DO NOW?
. . .

I WOULD CRAWL
ON MY FACE AND STOMACH
DOWN HER STREET.
AT NIGHT
TO BASK IN THE GLOW
OF THE STREET LAMP
OUTSIDE HER HOUSE
I WOULD.
I WOULD SLITHER
UP THE BRICK STAIRS
OF HER FRONT PORCH
AND REST MY CHIN AT THE TOP STEP
-- GAZING UP INTO HER ROOM
-- TV FLICKERING AGAINST THE WALL
-- SHADOWS
-- SHAPES
-- WALKING PAST THE WINDOW
OK
I'M TALKING SNAKEWISE
SUMMER LIKE
CHARMED?
YES.
I AM THAT
THERE I AM
ON HER STREET
ON HER PORCH

SOME DUDE COMES OUT
AND STEPS ON ME
SPLAT.
WHAT A DRAG.
. . .

KILL THE FATHER
FUCK THE MOTHER
EAT THE KIDS
BURN THE HOUSE DOWN
TAKE OVER
. . .

INSIDE:
THIRTEEN YEAR OLDS
SMOKING CIGARETTES
READING ROCK MAGAZINES
THEY ALL HAVE HIGH WATER PANTS
THE GUY BEHIND THE COUNTER
LOOKS LIKE CLARK KENT
OUTSIDE:
A GUY GETS OUT OF THE CAR
SAYS TO THE GIRL INSIDE
"WHAT KIND DO YOU WANT?"
I'M THINKING OF THAT POLICE CAR
ON PROSPECT

**UN-MANNED, PARKED, LIGHTS FLASHING**
**SOMEONE SHOULD TORCH IT**
**I CAN'T**
**ALL I'VE GOT IS A SNICKERS BAR**
**. . .**

**THE SUN IS DYING**
**LYING ON IT'S SIDE**
**ONE EYE OPEN**
**EVERY DAY**
**THE SUN DIES**
**IT COMMITS SUICIDE**
**DROWNS ITSELF**
**IN THE SEA**
**EVERY MORNING**
**THE SUN RISES**
**IT TEARS ACROSS THE SKY**
**JUST TO SHOW 'EM**
**I ASPIRE TO THAT**
**TO GIVE**
**TOTALLY**
**AND DIE EVERY NIGHT**
**AND THEN**
**TO BE GIVEN THE CHANCE**
**TO DIE AGAIN**
**SINKING**

**BURNING
DYING
AND RISING AGAIN
JUST TO SHOW 'EM
. . .**

**THE SUN DIED
I KILLED IT
RIPPED IT OUT OF THE SKY
CHOKED THE LIFE OUT OF IT
TURNED THE WORLD
COLD
BLACK
DEAD
AND IN NEED
TAKE CANDY FROM BABIES
STEP ON ANTS
IF YOU'RE IN LINE AT THE SUPERMARKET
KICK THE PEOPLE IN FRONT OF YOU
KICK YOUR WAY TO THE FRONT
LIE TO PEOPLE
SMILE AT THEM
AND THEN BASH THEIR SKULLS APART
WITH A CROWBAR
I AM A LITTLE OUT OF MY HEAD
PROBABLY TOO MUCH SUN.**

. . .

SITTING ALONE IN MY CELL AROUND 8:30 THE DEPRESSION COMES ROLLING IN. WRAPS ITSELF AROUND ME LIKE A BIG SNAKE, SUFFOCATING ME. TONIGHT WHEN IT GOT ME, I TURNED OUT THE LIGHT AND I SAT QUIETLY IN THE DARKNESS WAITING FOR IT TO SUBSIDE. SITTING ALONE, SITTING STILL. LISTENING TO THE RADIO. THINKING, WONDERING WHAT MY FATHER LOOKS LIKE NOW. HAVEN'T SEEN HIM IN ABOUT FIVE YEARS. I WOULD HEAR PEOPLE SAY: "I HAVEN'T SEEN MY OLD MAN FOR FIVE YEARS." NOW I'M ONE OF THEM. BIG SNAKE MADE OF LEAD, COILING AROUND ME, HOLDING ME DOWN. DAMN! I HATE WHEN THIS HAPPENS. I DON'T KNOW WHAT TO DO. IT GETS ME. TURNS ME COLD, LEADEN, MAKES ME WRITE, MAKES ME SING. DO DA, DO DA.

. . .

SLICING UP A CADAVER
NO PAIN
I TELL YOU

THE SHIT JUST DOESN'T HURT
KICKING A CORPSE
SINKING YOUR JACKBOOT
INTO MY SIDE.
THE RIBS CRACK
YOU CAN'T HURT ME
I DON'T FEEL IT
YOU CAN RAZOR ME UP
DISMEMBER ME
DISEMBOWEL ME
I WILL STILL OFFER YOU
MY HAND
I HOLD NO MALICE TOWARDS YOU
BECAUSE
VIOLENCE TOWARD MY FLESH
IS NOT THE KIND OF THING
THAT HURTS ME
THESE DAYS.

. . .

DANGLING CORPSE. IN COLD STORAGE. BIG STEEL HOOK THRU THE CORPSE'S THROAT. BARE LIGHT SENDS OUT HARSH, CRUDE RAYS. THEY DEFLECT OFF BLUISH, DEAD, CORPSE FLESH. AIN'T NUGHIN'! JUST COWS. I EAT EM', SMILING MEN AT

MCDONALD'S COOK 'EM. I WANT MORE MEANING TO MY FOOD MORE SOUL. SOME BOVINE, GRASS EATING ANIMAL JUST DON'T CUT THE MUSTARD WITH ME. LIKE I SAID, I NEED, I WANT, I GOTTA HAVE, MORE. I WANT. TO EAT. YOUR CHILDREN. JUST THE DAUGHTERS. I DON'T WANT TO EAT NO BOYS MAN, WHAT THE FUCK DO YOU THINK I AM? I SAW THAT LITTLE GIRL OUTSIDE THE LAUNDRY MAT ON ARTESIA BLVD. I WANTED ONE OF THOSE SLIM, TANNED, HAIRLESS LITTLE LEGS, MEDIUM WELL, WITH SOME GREY POUPON. SOUL FOOD. I DIG SOUL FOOD. I'M NOT A VEGETARIAN, I AM CARNIVOROUS, AN' I WANNA EAT YOUR FUCKING KID. BUT ONLY IF IT'S FEMALE! LIKE I SAID, I'M NO WEIRDO MAN. EAT THE LITTLE GIRLS, KILL THE LITTLE BOYS. THE STREETS ARE OPEN AIR MARKETS. PLAYGROUNDS ARE RESTAURANTS, PARKS WITH BUILT IN HIBACHIS ARE CONVENIENT AND VERY THOUGHTFUL.

. . .

GOD COMMITTED SUICIDE. BLEW HIS BRAINS OUT. ALL HELL BROKE LOOSE IN

HEAVEN. THE ANGELS STARTED FIGHTING OVER WHO WAS THE NEW BOSS. THE SKY STARTED TO FALL. DOWN ON EARTH, EVERYTHING WAS GOING SCREWY. PEOPLE WERE FREAKING OUT, RUNNING AROUND LIKE ANTS. GOD REALLY KNOCKED OVER THIS SHIT CAN THIS TIME. I SAT ON MY PATIO IN MALIBU, SIPPING A DAIQUIRI AND CHUCKLED AS LOS ANGELES BURNED. PEOPLE ARE STRANGE FOLKS.

. . .

THE SUN WILL RISE
THE SUN WILL BURN
THE TEARS
FROM YOUR EYES
THE SUN WILL RISE
THE SUN WILL BURN
DESIGNS IN YOU
SOME OF US
FIND STRENGTH
IN OUR WEAKNESSES
ARE DRIVEN INSANE
BY THE EYES OF THE SUN.
WHEN THEY STARE
DOWN

THE EYES OF THE SUN
BLIND ME IN MY DARKNESS
THERE IS STRENGTH
IN MY BLINDNESS
THERE IS LIGHT
BLINDING
SCORCHING
LIGHT
. . .

JACK
I COULD NEVER WALK THRU HER DOOR.
I WOULD HAVE TO TURN INTO A SNAKE
AND SLITHER UNDER THE DOOR. BUT
I WOULD CRAWL ON THE FLOOR FOR HER.
I WOULD.
I WOULD SLITHER ACROSS THE FLOOR
TO THE BED
I WOULD COIL MYSELF NEATLY
NEXT TO ONE OF HER LOVER'S SHOES
AND WAIT.
WHEN HE WOULD PUT HIS FOOT DOWN
I WOULD STRIKE
THEN TRY
TO TURN BACK INTO MY NORMAL SHAPE
BUT I COULD NEVER DO IT.

I WAS NEVER ONE OF HER LOVERS
I WAS A SNAKE
A CREATURE
CRAWLING
ON THE FLOOR
FOR HER
I WAS NEVER ONE OF HER LOVERS.
. . .

IN DISCIPLINE:
THE BLOOD ROARS
THE BRAIN TURNS TO MARBLE
THE MUSCLES TURN TO STEEL
WHEN WRAPPED IN THE SCALDING
ARMS OF THE DISCIPLINE:
I CAN'T RIP MY EYES AWAY FROM
THE SUN
I FEEL NO PAIN
IF YOU KNOW WHAT I MEAN
THEN YOU KNOW WHAT I MEAN
. . .

I AM STARTING TO THINK THAT I AM NOT A HUMAN BEING. I DON'T FEEL LIKE ONE, I THINK I WAS ONE WHEN I WAS ABOUT 17 OR SOMETHING. NOW I REALLY THINK I AM

SOMETHING ELSE. I DON'T BELONG HERE. MAYBE I AM A SNAKE, A COPPER SNAKE, DUSTY, ADDICTED, CRAWLING SLOWLY. I DO NOT SUFFER. ONLY WOUNDED SUFFER. I AM NOT WOUNDED. I AM INFLICTED, RATHER, I INFLICT MYSELF UPON MYSELF. I RE-ARRANGE, BREAKDOWN, DEPLETE MYSELF OF MYSELF, CAUSING HUNGER, CAUSING PAIN. PEOPLE HATE PEOPLE WHO ARE FREE. PEOPLE WHO ARE WAITING FOR THEIR "REWARD" WILL WAIT FOREVER, CONTENT TO HATE, FEAR AND CONDEMN. I AM UP TO OTHER THINGS IN THE MEAN TIME. FREAKY, MISFITS, DISCIPLES OF THE SUN, YOU ARE THE ONES WHO UNDERSTAND THE RHYTHM OF DISEASE. THE COLD, ISOLATING, BEAUTIFUL FIRE OF THE DISTORTED SOUL. THE FLOWERS BLOOM FOR YOU! THE BIRDS IN THE SKY SING FOR YOU! THE SUN SHINES FOR YOU! THE COPPER SNAKE CRAWLS FOR YOU.

. . .

SHE TOUCHES ME
(THE JUNGLE LIGHTS UP WITH AN
INCINERATING FIRE, LOOKS LIKE

A FLAMING SERPENT)
I LOOK INTO HER EYES
I SEE A MOVIE FLICKERING
CAR CRASHES
PEOPLE KICKING CORPSES
MEN RIPPING THEIR TRACHEAS OUT
AND SHAKING THEM AT THE SKY
I THINK TO MYSELF: I DON'T WANT
TO SURVIVE THIS ONE.
I WANT TO BURN UP
IN THE WRECKAGE.
COOKING FLESH IN THE JUNGLE.
. . .

DRINK
ALOT
GET DRUNK ALOT AND WORK 40 HOURS A
WEEK
SPEND 15 TO 20 HOURS
HUNG OVER
SICK
WEAK
UNABLE TO HANDLE
SOMEHOW
MAKE YOURSELF THINK THAT THIS IS COOL
AND THAT YOU HAVE NO CHOICE

AND THAT "THEY DRIVE ME TO IT."
AND THAT YOU CAN "QUIT ANY TIME I WANT"
THERE
YOU'RE LIVING IN HELL.

. . .

I'VE SEEN TOO MANY DRUNKS TONITE.
THEY STUMBLE AROUND THE LIVING ROOM
REEKING
OF BEER & CIGARETTES
TALKING BULLSHIT
TALKING IN MY FACE
TO ME
MAKING ME
SMELL THEIR GOOD TIME
WASTING
MY GOOD TIME
AND MAKING TIME DRAG
AND MAKING TIME
DRAG
WHAT
A
DRAG

. . .

MY FATHER TOLD ME THAT BLACKS ARE CALLED SPADES. HE TOLD ME THAT EVERY GOOD SPADE WAS A DEAD SPADE. HE TOLD ME NEVER TO MAKE FAG JOKES OUTSIDE THE HOUSE OR SOMEONE MIGHT THINK I WAS GAY AND THIS WAS WORSE THAN DEATH. HE SAID MY MOM WAS A SPADE LOVER AND I SHOULDN'T BE BECAUSE SHE WAS JUST A WOMAN AND DIDN'T KNOW ANYTHING REALLY. HE SAID THAT A DEMOCRAT IS A LIBERAL WHO'S BEEN MUGGED. HE TOLD ME THAT MARTIN LUTHER KING IS A GOOD SPADE.

. . .

SOME PEOPLE ARE CRITICS. THEY CAN TELL YOU WHAT'S IN A MAN'S SOUL BY JUST TURNING ON THEIR TYPEWRITERS. THEY TAKE THEIR BULLSHIT EGO TRIPS AND PUT DOWN PEOPLE WHO GET MORE STUFF DONE THAN THEM. THEY TYPE OUT SHIT THAT YOU CAN READ AND UNDERSTAND, YOU AND THE CRITIC ARE USUALLY ON THE SAME LEVEL, WHETHER YOU AGREE WITH EACH OTHER OR NOT, DO YOU DIG WHAT I'M SAYING? SOME "DO IT" AND SOME JUST

MAKE THEIR LIVING BY WRITING ABOUT
PEOPLE THAT "DO IT." I'M GLAD I'M NOT IN
THAT BULLSHIT GAME AND BY THE WAY
FUCK YOU.
. . .

GET ON THE CINDER TRAIL
SEE THE INDIAN MAN
TURN AROUND
FEEL THE SUN
FEEL THE FORKED TONGUE
BURN IN YOUR MOUTH
TURN AROUND
SEE ME AWAKENING FROM A
NIGHT'S SLEEP ON AN INDIAN
BURIAL MOUND, IN AN INDIAN
BURIAL GROUND. SOAKING UP DEATH
TURN AROUND
WHAT DO YOU SEE?
THE SKY IS FULL OF FIRE
THE RAIN WILL BURN YOU DOWN
YOU SPAT WHEN YOU SAW ME
WHEN YOU SAW YOUR FACE MIRRORED IN
MINE
TURN AROUND, IT'S JUST A CIRCLE
TURN AROUND.

IT ONLY TAKES A SECOND
TO OPEN YOUR EYES
TO REALIZE YOUR CIRCLE
TURN AROUND.

. . .

WHAT IF YOU TOOK A PERSON WHO LOVED TO KILL AND PUT THAT PERSON IN A ROOM WITH A PERSON WHO LOVED TO DIE AND TOLD THEM TO "MAKE LOVE"? WOULD THAT BE OK? MURDER IS ILLEGAL. IF THE PERSON WHO LOVED TO KILL GOT LIFE IMPRISONMENT, THEN HE WOULD BE PUNISHED FOR HIS LOVE. DOES THAT MEAN I GET TO BLOW UP A CHURCH DURING A MARRIAGE CEREMONY TO PUNISH THE BRIDE AND GROOM FOR THEIR LOVE? WOULDN'T I BE DOING A PUBLIC SERVICE? I'M SO CONFUSED!

. . .

THE MEN ARE OUT TONIGHT
LOOKING FOR YOUR CHILDREN
WADING THRU CREEKS
TALKING INTO WALKIE-TALKIES
SMOKING MARLBOROUGHS

**POKING THE LEAVES
HOPING TO FIND
SHALLOW GRAVES
HOPING THAT
THEIR STICKS WILL POKE
SMALL
ROTTING
CORPSES
YES
I TOOK THEM INTO THE WOODS
BEHIND MY FATHER'S HOUSE
I BASHED AND CHOKED THEM
IN A ROCK GARDEN
I COULDN'T LET THEM GROW UP
TO BE POLICEMEN
FATHERS
MOTHERS
DRUNKS IN FAST CARS
I COULDN'T LET THEM GROW UP TO BE YOU
I SAW ONE OF YOUR TELEVISION SHOWS.
A MAN SAID "LET'S DO IT TO THEM BEFORE
THEY DO IT TO US"
THAT SOUNDED LIKE GOOD ADVICE.
SO I'M "DOING IT"
TO YOU
TO YOURS**

I HATE YOUR HATRED
YOUR PAIN HURTS ME
THE TRUTH IS THAT YOUR LIES ARE
"DOING IT" TO ME
YOUR WORLD IS
"DOING IT" TO ME
SO
I TOOK YOUR ADVICE
AND NOW
I'M "DOING IT" TOO.
. . .

DEAD
OVEN
COME INTO THE OVEN
CRAWL INTO THE OVEN
I'LL WAIT
THE VULTURES ARE CLAWING
THE ROOF
IN THE OVEN
IT GETS SO
HOT
HOT
HOT
AND I BURN
WHITE

**HOT**
**WHITE**
**HOT**
**I'VE BEEN BURNING FOREVER**
**BURNING OVER AND OVER**
**BURNING**
**WHITE**
**HOT**
**I CRAWLED IN HERE TO DIE**
**I CRAWLED OUT OF ONE HOLE**
**AND INTO THIS**
**AND I CAN HEAR THE VULTURES**
**CLAWING AT THE ROOF**
**AND I BURN**
**WHITE HOT**
**. . .**

**COULD YOU LOVE MY GOUGED OUT SKULL-HEAD? COULD YOU LOVE MY REMAINS AFTER THEY WERE DRAGGED OUT OF THE ACID BATH? MY REMAINS WERE DRAGGED OUT OF THE ACID BATH AND LAID OUT ON THE FLOOR, MY BODY WAS TORN, EATEN AWAY. I AM MISSHAPEN. I DON'T EVEN FEEL ANY PAIN. PLEASE LOVE ME SO I CAN FEEL THE PAIN AGAIN. I FEEL SO PAINLESS**

SOMETIMES THAT I THINK THAT I AM DEAD. BORED OUT, LYING ON THE FLOOR. NOT EVEN HUMAN ANY MORE.

. . .

SOME TIMES WHEN THE COLD WIND BLOWS MY WAY, I DON'T EVEN NEED A COAT BECAUSE I JUST CAN'T EVEN FEEL IT, MAN, I JUST DON'T EVEN KNOW. IT PROBABLY BLOWS THRU ME. IT'S LIKE FREEZING A CORPSE, IT DOESN'T EVEN KNOW THAT IT'S ASS IS FREEZING OFF. GODDAMN, SOME TIMES IT GETS SO COLD IN HERE, WHEN I FEEL IT, WHEN I DON'T FEEL IT, I HURT WORSE, AND THAT SHIT HURTS.

. . .

I SEE SUNSHINE
I SEE CLEAR SKY
I SEE PALM TREES
I SEE THE OCEAN
I FEEL THE OCEAN BREEZE
I SEE 7-11
I SEE BURGER KING
I FEEL THE FAMINE
I SEE THE DISEASE

I SAY: "DOUBLE DOUBLE CHEESE CHEESE BURGER BURGER PLEASE"
I SEE THE BODY BAGS PILED UP IN THE STREETS
I SEE THE TRUCKS COME
TO HAUL
THE DEAD BODIES AWAY
TO THEIR INCINERATION
SURF'S UP
. . .

WHEN YOU TAKE A FEMALE CHILD INTO THE BACK YARD. WHEN YOU SNAP IT'S SPINE WITH YOUR HANDS, WHEN YOU DECAPITATE THE CORPSE, WHEN YOU CUT OPEN IT'S STOMACH AND CLEAN OUT THE STEAMING ENTRAILS INTO A BUCKET, WHEN YOU INSERT A SKEWER THRU THE ANUS THAT EXITS THRU THE NECK-STUMP, WHEN YOU TIE THE LITTLE HANDS AND ARMS BACK, WHEN YOU PUT THE CORPSE OVER THE COALS AND START TO TURN IT, AROUND AND AROUND, WHEN THE SKIN IS CHARRED BLACK AND JUICE IS DRIPPING OFF THE CORPSE ONTO THE HISSING COALS, IT

DOESN'T EVEN LOOK HUMAN ANY MORE.
NOT HUMAN. ANYMORE.
. . .

CRUCIFY THE RATS!
DEIFY THE ROACHES!
CANONNIZE DISEASE!
DON'T FORGET THE FLIES
BAPTIZE
THE FLIES
OR THEY WILL EAT OUT
YOUR EYES
DON'T FORGET
THE FLIES
RIDE IN DADDY'S STATION WAGON
INFLICT
THE DIVINE PUNISHMENT
HAIL!
THE DIVINE PUNISHMENT
CRAWL
CRAWL
YEA
DON'T FORGET THE FLIES
HAIL!
SAINT PLAGUE

. . .

BURNING LIGHT
SHINING BRIGHT
ANNIHILATING
THE DARKNESS
IN MY BRAIN
YOU SEE MYSELF
STARING THRU TO YOUR SOUL
AND YOU MIGHT
THINK THAT I AM
INSANE
AND YOU MIGHT BE RIGHT
. . .

I HAVE LEARNED ALOT IN THE LAST FEW WEEKS. I HAVE LEARNED TO QUESTION SMILING FACES. I DON'T TRUST SMILING FACES ANYMORE. WHEN SOMEONE SMILES AND REACHES OUT TO SHAKE MY HAND, I TRY AND GUESS WHAT THEY WANT FROM ME AND WHEN THEY WILL TRY TO SINK THE KNIFE IN. IT'S SO EASY TO GET PULLED IN ON A CONFIDENCE SCAM. YOU FEEL SHOCKED AND AMAZED THAT A PERSON YOU WERE HELPING WAS JUST GETTING OVER ON YOU. HE'S SHAKING YOUR HAND

AND PULLING YOU INTO YOUR GRAVE. WHEN SOMEONE GIVES SOMETHING AWAY, THEY WANT SOMETHING IN RETURN, SOME HOW, SOME WAY. THIS IS A GAME THAT GETS PLAYED ON MANY LEVELS. DON'T TAKE CANDY FROM STRANGERS UNLESS YOU'RE WILLING TO TAKE A RIDE IN THE CAR.

. . .

I TRY TO SMILE WHEN PEOPLE TALK TO ME BUT I CAN FEEL THE REFRIGERATION MAN BEHIND MY FLESH. I CAN'T LET THEM KNOW THE FACE I SEE. I CHASE MYSELF. I ALWAYS CATCH UP. I NEVER DENY. I TRY TO AVOID. MYSELF. I AM DESTROYING MYSELF TO GIVE BIRTH TO MY SOUL. THE OTHER NIGHT I FELT VIOLENT PAIN IN MY STOMACH. SOMETHING WAS INSIDE ME. MY STOMACH CONTRACTED AND I THOUGHT I WAS GOING TO VOMIT. I FELT SOMETHING CRAWLING UP MY THROAT. I OPENED MY MOUTH. A LARGE, GREASY, BLACK RAT SQUIRMED OUT AND FELL ON THE FLOOR. IT QUIVERED FOR A MOMENT AND CRAWLED AWAY. I GAVE BIRTH. THE MAN BEHIND MY

FACE TELLS ME TO SMILE, TELLS ME TO SPEAK. WHEN I AM ALONE, THE ROACHES COME OUT OF MY PORES, I GIVE BIRTH TO RATS. I CATCH UP WITH MY SELF. I PULL AWAY FROM THE FACE THAT SMILES AND ACTS AND TALKS. I AM DESTROYING MYSELF.

. . .

I AM DYING OF HATE. SUFFOCATING. FIST OVER FIST POUNDING DOWN ON MY HEAD. I AM DYING OF HATE. I GOT MY HANDS WRAPPED AROUND MY THROAT AND I AM SQUEEZING MY SELF SHUT. I AM TRYING TO CLOSE MY WOUNDS. I AM DYING OF HATE. I FEEL UGLY. I AM DYING OF HATE. I DON'T WANT TO SEE LIGHT AGAIN. I DON'T WANT TO HEAR THOSE SOUNDS AGAIN. I AM DYING OF HATE. A CIRCLE IN A SQUARE. THE LINES ARE STRAIGHT BUT THE EDGES ARE SMOOTH AND THERE ARE NO ANSWERS HERE.

. . .

THE FIRST TIME I TOOK LSD, I CAME ON AT A BURGER KING. I WAS SITTING IN THIS

GIRL'S CAR ABOUT TO EAT THIS DOUBLE WHOPPER AND IT HIT ME. ALL OF A SUDDEN I THOUGHT THAT THIS WARM THING I WAS CUPPING IN MY HANDS WAS AN INFANT'S HEAD. AT FIRST I THOUGHT I COULD NOT DO THAT, I COULDN'T EAT A BABIES BRAINS, NO WAY. BUT I DID. EVERY BITE I TOOK, I COULD SEE EVERY PART OF THE HEAD THAT I WAS EATING MEAT JUICE DRIPPED DOWN MY CHIN. THERE I WAS EATING THIS KID'S HEAD, KID OF LIKE AN ALL MEAT GRAPEFRUIT. I ATE EVERY BITE. LIFE IS A LOOSENING PROCESS. THINGS YOU THOUGHT YOU WOULD NEVER DO BEFORE GET DONE WHEN YOU GET RID OF THOSE INHIBITIONS THAT HANG YOU UP. SO TAKE MY ADVICE AND LOOSEN UP A LITTLE OK!

. . .

WHITE BOY. DOG EYE. WHITE BOY. GLOWING, WALKING DOWN THE STREET, HANDS IN POCKET, SKIN GLOWING. INSANE. SMILING, GOING DOWN TO THE PUBLIC POOL TO SWIM IN THE PISS WATER. GOING DOWN TO GET BEAT UP. DOG BRAIN.

**WHITE BOY SENDING OUT VIBES: TAKE MY MONEY, SCARE ME SO MY KNEES KNOCK TOGETHER. BASH MY MOUTH INTO THE WATER FOUNTAIN. I KNOW I DON'T DESERVE TO LIVE. WHITE BOY SWEATING OFF IVORY SOAP IN THE SUMMER HEAT. WHITE BOY WITH BUS TOKEN SAFETY PINNED ONTO T-SHIRT. WHITE, SCARED AND TRAPPED. SEALED INSIDE A BOTTLE OF AUGUST HEAT.**

**. . .**

**I AM FOLLOWED. EVERYWHERE I GO. I AM FOLLOWED BY CANCER MAN. HE TOUCHES ME AND I BRUISE. I FEEL WEAK WHEN HE IS NEAR. FROM NIGHT TO NIGHT, FROM CLUB TO CLUB HE FOLLOWS ME. HE BREATHES ON ME. HE MAKES ME LONELY, HE MAKES ME WANT FOR HUMAN KINDNESS. HE STARVES MY SOUL. HE STEALS MY SANITY. I HATE CANCER MAN FOR THE EMPTINESS HE FILLS ME WITH. HE LAYS NEXT TO ME AT NIGHT AND MAKES ME FEEL THE BOTTOM OF MY HEART OVER AND OVER AGAIN. HE IS IN THE AUDIENCE EVERY NIGHT, SUCKING ME DRY, MAKING ME WANT**

FOR A HUMAN TOUCH AND MAKING SURE IT NEVER COMES. HE IS VERY CLOSE NOW, VERY CLOSE, SO CLOSE. I AM CANCER MAN. TURNING MYSELF CHARRED AND LIFELESS. I AM CANCER MAN. I HATE CANCER MAN.

. . .

THEY SMILE
THEY WILL HURT YOU
TURN INSIDE
YOUR ONLY FRIEND IS INSIDE
THEY WILL CUT YOUR HEART
THEY WILL MAIM YOUR SOUL
I NEED SOMEONE SO BAD
I THINK I AM GOING TO BREAK INTO
LITTLE PIECES.
YOU CANNOT TOUCH
YOU CANNOT BE TOUCHED
YOU ARE DIRTY AND INSANE
YOU COME FROM A DIFFERENT PLANET
NO ONE WILL EVER UNDERSTAND
EVER
TURN INSIDE
REMEMBER
WHAT ALWAYS HAPPENS

A BARE BULB BURNS IN AN APARTMENT IN MY BRAIN. IN THE MIDDLE OF THE APARTMENT IS A SMALL TABLE AND A WOODEN CHAIR. THERE IS A COT IN THE CORNER. PACING THE FLOOR OF THE APARTMENT IS A MAN WHO HAS NEVER SLEPT, EVER. HE STARES OUT THE WINDOW CONSTANTLY. HE IS SCARRED AND INSANE FROM HIS THOUGHTS. EVERYTHING HE THINKS IS TRUE. THAT'S WHY HE LIVES ALONE. HE WRITES WORDS ON THE WALLS TO REMIND AND CONSOLE HIMSELF:
ALIENATION
HARD ROAD
INCINERATE
NEVER
HEART ACHE
SOUL
FOREVER
. . .

WE NEED TO SPEND MORE TIME IN THE DARKNESS. YES WE DO. YOU AND ME, GIRL. DARKNESS SMOOTHES THINGS OVER.

THE SOUL IS LET FREE TO BE EMBRACED. COME TO ME IN DARKNESS. YOU WILL SEE ME. YOU WILL UNDERSTAND ME. YOU WILL TOUCH MY DESPERATION. IN DARKNESS WE ARE SECRETS. IN DARKNESS WE ARE EVERY THING, WE ARE SAFE, SEALED OFF FROM THE FILTHY LIGHT THAT DEFILES US AND LEAVES US LIFELESS AND COLD. TOUCH ME IN DARKNESS. CALL MY NAME AND I WILL COME TO YOU. IN DARKNESS YOU WILL SEE THAT WE ARE EVERYTHING.

. . .

DEAR _____

I HEARD THIS DUDE TELL ABOUT HOW HE GOT A HOOKER AND PAID HER TO SUCK HIS COCK. SHE PUT A RUBBER ON HIS COCK AND WENT FOR IT. HE WAS TOO DRUNK TO COME IN THE RUBBER THAT WAS IN THE WOMAN'S MOUTH. I DON'T KNOW WHY I THOUGHT OF THAT RIGHT NOW BUT THE IDEA OF SOME ART STUDENT SITTING IN HIS VW GETTING HEAD FROM A HOOKER AND NOT BEING ABLE TO COME IS KINDA FUNNY.

HAVING FUN WISH YOU WERE HERE WITH ME.
. . .

TODAY I FEEL ON THE OUTSIDE OF EVERYTHING WHERE DOES THAT PUT ME? INSIDE? INSIDE OF ME? TODAY, RIGHT NOW I FEEL ON THE OUTSIDE OF THAT TOO. ON THE OUTSIDE OF THE OUTSIDE. ROLLING OVER AND PLAYING DEAD SO NO ONE WILL NOTICE. I DID AN "APPEARANCE" AT A RECORD STORE TODAY. I COULD NOT RELATE TO THOSE PEOPLE. NOT AT ALL. FUCK, I DON'T KNOW.
. . .

SITTING IN THE BACK ROOM OF A CLUB IN THE SOUTH.
COLD, SWEATY, STINKING FROM DIRT AND SWEAT.
THINKING ABOUT THE THINGS THAT DROVE ME INSANE.
SILENCE.
BLINDING BEAUTY
THE SUN
THE BRUTAL DESERT

STARING AT A PERFECT,
BLOND, CUNT, JUST INCHES
AWAY FROM MY FACE.
HER BREATHING, HOT ON
MY FACE
THE FEELING OF WANTING
TO DIE EVERY TIME IT'S
GOOD.
AND WANTING IT TO BE GOOD
SO BAD.
. . .

MY DEAREST, TO LIVE OUT THERE, YOU MUST HAVE EYES THAT ACT AS PRISMS, TO DISMANTLE AND REFRACT ANYTHING THAT COMES BEFORE THEM. YOU MUST HAVE SKIN AS HARD AND AS SEAMLESS AS GLASS. MORE LIKE ELASTIC MARBLE. YES. A HARD EXTERIOR IS A MUST. THEIR TALK, THEIR EYES, THEIR TRUE MOTIVES, ARE LIKE SAND FILLED WIND. WEARING YOU DOWN. TAKING AWAY YOUR EDGE, MAKING YOU MALLEABLE, SO SLOWLY AND EVENLY THAT YOU WON'T REALIZE IT UNTIL IT'S TOO LATE. IT'S ONLY BECAUSE YOU BROUGHT MY BLOOD TO A BOIL, ONLY BECAUSE YOU

LOOKED INTO MY HEART AND TOUCHED MY SOUL ONLY BECAUSE YOU GAVE YOURSELF TO ME COMPLETELY THAT I TELL YOU THIS. GET A LOCK FOR YOUR DOOR. THEY ARE EVERY WHERE. REMAIN INTACT. I WILL BE WITH YOU AGAIN.

. . .

I AM THE DISMEMBERED MAN WALKING DISLOCATED AND STIFF, WHITE SKIN GLOWING. SENDING OFF BLUISH LIGHT. LOOKING AND FEELING UNNATURAL, EVERYWHERE I GO. SEE ME AT THE BEACH WALKING AROUND LIKE AN ASSHOLE ON HOLIDAY, TALKING LOUD AND COVERING UP MY TRACKS WITH OATHS AND BEER. AT THE END OF THE DAY I AM RED AND SWOLLEN AND ALL TIRED OUT FROM FIGHTING WITH THE FLIES.

. . .

WHEN SHE COMES:
SHE PULLS YOU CLOSE
SHE BREATHES IN SHORT BURSTS
HER EYES CLOSE
HER HEAD TILTS BACK

HER MOUTH OPENS SLIGHTLY
HER THIGHS TURN TO STEEL AND THEN MELT
SHE IS PERFECT
AND YOU FEEL LIKE YOU ARE EVERYTHING
. . .

WHENEVER I AM IN MY HOME TOWN, I AM REMINDED OF MY FATHER. I MIGHT HAVE BREATHED THE SAME AIR HE HAD JUST A DAY BEFORE. I CAN FEEL HIM. I CAN FEEL HIS BREATHING. I CAN FEEL HIS HEART BEAT. I THINK OF THE DISCIPLINE. THE INSTRUCTION. THE THINGS HE SAID. THE FEAR AND ANGUISH AND HATRED. I WALK ON THE SAME STREETS AS HE DOES. HIS FOOT PRINTS GLOW IN THE DARK. HE GOT ME GOOD AND IT MAKES ME WANT TO KILL.
. . .

HOW ABOUT
TAKING SOME DRUGS
GETTING HIGH
HOW ABOUT
GETTING NAKED
HOWS ABOUT

**KILLING SOME PIGS
HOW ABOUT
A BURNING KNIFE
COMING DOWN
FROM THE SKY
RIGHT INTO YOUR BRAIN
HOW ABOUT
LIVING IN THE BOTTOM OF THE DRAIN?
HOWS ABOUT
EATING TEN MILES OF PUSSY
HOW ABOUT SUCKING
SOME FINE, FINE DICK
HOW ABOUT
GETTING LOOSE
HOW ABOUT
FEELING GOOD
HOW ABOUT
FEELING NO PAIN
HOW ABOUT
A SYRINGE
CRAWLING IN YOUR VEIN
HOW ABOUT NEVER COMING BACK
AND DRIVING YOURSELF INSANE
HOW ABOUT THE MISSION
OF THE SWASTIKA BRAIN?
HOW ABOUT LOVE**

HOWS ABOUT DISCIPLINE
HOWS ABOUT EYES THAT BURN RIGHT THRU
HOW ABOUT LIVING ALL THE TIME?
HOW ABOUT IT?
. . .

THERE ARE NIGHTS WHERE I CANNOT SLEEP
THEY HAPPEN ALL THE TIME.
IN THESE PERIODS, I DON'T WANT TO EXIST
WOULDN'T IT BE NICE
TO BE NO ONE
RIGHT NOW?
WHEN I AM LYING THERE, I ALWAYS THINK
OF TWO
THINGS.
CUNT
AND SUICIDE
WOULDN'T IT BE NICE
TO BE NO ONE
RIGHT NOW?
SOMETIMES I WILL LIE THERE AND HOPE
THAT I WILL DIE
RIGHT THEN. I DON'T WANT TO EXIST. NO
BIG DEAL. NO
BIG SOB STORY. I DON'T MAKE A FUCKING
SOUND. I JUST

DON'T WANT IT ANY MORE AND NOTHING
CAN PULL ME
BACK.
WOULDN'T IT BE NICE TO BE NO ONE RIGHT
NOW?
I WAIT FOR SLEEP
TO TAKE ME
TO STOP ME FROM THINKING
TO RID ME OF ME
WOULDN'T IT BE NICE TO BE NO ONE RIGHT
NOW?
. . .

I WANT TO BE HERE FOR YOU.
I WANT TO BE REAL FOR YOU
AM I REAL?
I DON'T KNOW
HELP ME
HELP ME KNOW THAT I AM REAL
I DON'T KNOW WHAT I AM
AM I ALIVE?
AM I HERE.
TELL ME
SHOW ME
TOUCH ME
MAKE ME EXIST

. . .

**FOLLOW THE SNAKE.
HE LEAVES A TRAIL
THAT GLOWS IN THE SAND
WHEN YOU LEARN TO CRAWL
THE TRAIL IS SO EASY TO UNDERSTAND.
FOR A LOVE THAT WILL NEVER LEAVE YOU.
AND FOR A SOUL THAT NEVER DIES.
YOU DON'T HAVE TO LIVE FOREVER.
TO FINALLY REALIZE,
THE MUSIC OF THE SKY.
THE SCREAM OF THE SUN
AND THE CRAWL OF THE SNAKE.
LIMBLESS
PERFECT
AND ABSOLUTE
CRAWL.**

. . .

**SWIRLING ABOVE HIS BODY NOW
I FIND A WORLD AWAY FROM HIS PAIN
I'M LIVING AND DYING
IN ANOTHER BRAIN
IN THE MIND OF A SNAKE
I AM COLD AND DUSTY**

BUT ALIVE
AND THAT'S GOOD ENOUGH
IN THIS REPTILE HOUSE
IF I AM ALIVE
I WILL SURVIVE
AND I WILL CRAWL THIS TRAIL
UNTIL MY BELLY BLEEDS
AND THEN I'LL CRAWL IT SOME MORE
CRAWL.
. . .

I HAVE WATCHED YOUR PEOPLE FOR A VERY LONG TIME. I HAVE BEEN TAKING VERY THOROUGH NOTES AND I HAVE BEEN MAKING VOCAL ENTRIES INTO MY TAPE RECORDER. I HAVE BEEN CHRONICLING EVERY VICE, EVERY FEAR, EVERY WEAKNESS. EVERY ONE. I HAVE WEAPONS. I WILL USE THESE AGAINST YOU. I WILL REFLECT YOU AT YOURSELF. YOU TEACH ME SO MUCH ABOUT YOURSELF. YOUR AVERSION TO THE TRUTH AND YOUR FEAR OF REJECTION AND FAILURE MAKE YOU EASY. I WATCH YOU FROM ABOVE. I WILL STRIKE WHEN YOU ARE AT YOUR LOWEST, WEAKEST LEVEL. SEE YOU AROUND.

. . .

THIS IS THE HOUSE WHERE YOU
SPENT ALL THOSE YEARS
THIS IS THE HOUSE WHERE YOU
LEARNED SO MUCH
THIS IS THE HOUSE THAT WAS
HOME
THE PLACE THAT DEFINES HOME
WITH ALL THE WARMTH AND
COMFORT THAT GOES ALONG
WITH THE THOUGHT OF HOME.
THIS IS THE PLACE THAT YOU
THOUGHT WOULD LAST FOREVER.
THIS IS THE PLACE YOU THOUGHT
YOU WOULD NEVER LEAVE
OR WANT TO
THIS IS THE PLACE THAT YOU
WILL SOMEDAY WANT TO BURN TO
THE GROUND.

. . .

I WORK AT A DINER
I DON'T HATE THIS JOB
I DON'T HATE ANYTHING
I DON'T KNOW MY NAME

I'M FACELESS
I LOOK AT THEM
THEY LOOK AT ME
I HEARD ABOUT MYSELF IN A
BRUCE SPRINGSTEEN SONG
I AM NO ONE
I AM FACELESS
I DON'T KNOW WHAT TO DO
I COME HERE AND THEN I GO HOME
I FEEL SO BLANK TODAY
AM I HERE?
DO I EXIST?
HELP ME
I AM TURNING TO WOOD.

. . .

I AM WAITING
I AM WAITING TO BE MELTED
I AM WAITING FOR THE CORN TO RIPEN IN
ITS PODS
I AM WAITING TO BE TOUCHED
I AM WAITING TO HAVE MY NAME CALLED.
I DON'T KNOW WHAT MY NAME IS
BUT WHEN SHE CALLS IT, I'LL KNOW
I AM WAITING TO BE ASKED
I AM WAITING FOR THE SUN TO EXPLODE

**I AM WAITING FOR THE FLOWERS TO RIP OPEN
I AM WAITING TO BE TOUCHED
I AM WAITING
BEYOND SILENCE
BEYOND PATIENCE
BEYOND TIME**
. . .

I am walking down a street. I cross the street. A car nearly runs me over as it ploughs through the stop sign. No respect. A pig works security at a show in his off duty hours and threatens and harasses the owner of the club that he is working for. No respect. A car waves me over, the driver says "Aren't you Henry Rollins?" I say yes, he says "Playing tomorrow night?" I say yes. He flips me off and drives away. No respect. People will suck your blood until you dry up and blow away. No respect there.

This is for the girl's Daddy: Hey, Daddy, you made a fine daughter, you and your wife should be proud. She is so fine. Daddy. She is blonde, 18 years old, slim, great tits.

Checked out those melons lately, Daddy? Lord have mercy! They look so ripe and fine, like peaches on a pretty peach tree. Daddy, your girl sucks cock real good. How do I know this Daddy? Because she was in a back room of a club, sucking on my cock. You should have seen us Daddy, I had my back against the wall and that girl was on her knees sucking my cock. I stared down and watched her pretty little head go up and down, up and down, I looked at her knees, grinding into that greasy, filthy, rancid floor and I thought of you. Finally, I came. I came right into her mouth Daddy. She was into it. Every drop. She stroked my cock to squeeze out every last drop of my cum, which she swallowed. That must have been a real drag for her boyfriend, who was waiting outside in the hallways. Oh well, what he doesn't know won't hurt him, but I hope it does anyway. Daddy, during all that bliss, I forgot your daughter's name, but it's cool Pops, because I don't give a fuck. No respect.

. . .

I got a letter from my dead father's mother the other day. She sent me a book of Russian poetry called Red Cats. I threw it away because it was touched by the woman who bore my father. I should have used more caution. I could have caught a disease. Filthy animal. I read her letter, she told me that before my father died he told her that Black Flag has several "items" for sale, she wanted to know where she could get herself some. At the very moment I read that, I had a vision of my father's corpse, hanging gutted and cleaned in a meat locker. His corpse had a steel hook plunged through the back of the neck, the tip of the hook protruded through his Adam's apple, he looked a bit confused just hanging there. I remember beating his dead body with a 2x4, his body bucked and swung wildly with every blow. He was kind of like a flesh pinata. I beat him until it just plain bored me. Then I cut his body down and butchered him. I packed the meat in ice and sold the lot of it out of my car trunk in lower class districts of his home town. I took the money and bought some pussy and some drugs and a new gun.

I threw the letter away and went about my business. It's funny how things work out.
. . .

It's 4:23 a.m. I cannot sleep. I feel so distraught and I cannot sleep. I roll to my left side and then to my right. No luck. I am sinking so deep into myself that I cannot get out. I imagine myself in a jungle, wandering around, looking for a break in the trees. There is none yet. I sat on the front porch for a while, now I'm back inside the house.
WHAT ABOUT,
THOSE LONG NIGHTS SPENT ALONE
UNABLE TO SLEEP
SITTING VERY STILL
SITTING VERY QUIETLY
WITH YOUR HEAD IN YOUR HANDS
NOT A SOUL AROUND TO WATCH YOU BURN
THAT'S SOME REAL BAD BLUES
ALONE
TORN UP
EMPTY
WITH YOUR HEAD IN YOUR HANDS
YOU FEEL LIKE DYING
YES YOU DO

The alienation inside me is growing all the time. I just can't identify. It hurts. Who will be next to one of them? I am helpless I am alone. It hurts to feel this. It hurts even more to know I am right. I feel on the outside of everything except myself and it's in myself where I choke and drown. I cannot sleep tonight. If my shoes didn't hurt so much I'd go for a long walk, but I can't. The sound of their voices is maddening, the more they talk to me, the more they push me away from them and into myself.

I AM THE VACUUM MAN
BREATHING IN PAIN
EYES SUCKING INWARD
PORES CLOSING OFF
SKULL CLENCHING IN ON BRAIN
TURNING INWARD
BLEEDING
INTERNAL BLEEDING
RUPTURING
LIVING INSIDE THE VACUUM
SILENT
VACANT
BOTTOMLESS
CONSUMING

**TURNING INWARD
BEHIND THE GLASS CURTAIN
GOING BLIND
AND EVENTUALLY CAVING IN**

It reaches the point where the faces and the sounds bring pain to me. I will never break through. When I move forward (what I think is forward) I get knocked back immeasurable distances, and with this flight comes clear realization of the jungle that I live in. A move forward is idiocy. Pure idiocy. There must be a part of me that hates me, to make me go out and cut myself like that. There is music in my head. Music that won't let me be. The music is at a horrendous din. Deafening. Why do they turn on you like that, why do they let you down and push you out and shut you in? Why do they make you hurt until the point of numbness and collapse? Why do they do it? How do they do it? How do I do it, do it to myself, why do I do it to myself? Please, help me break it down. Touch me, no don't. I'm sorry, touch me, please, I need, I need, I need, I ...

. . .

I am confused. People really make me spin out. Damn them for that! Last night I was playing, and there were people coming up and touching me and grabbing me the whole night. This is not unusual, it happens all the time. Last night it hit me that I do not understand the difference between this kind of adulation and affection of a girl I want to be with, who wants to be with me. If you have a few hundred people call your name and poke at you all the time, you might not value it, or maybe not consider it real anymore. If someone tied me up and started whipping me, there would come a point where I would not feel it anymore. That's what I am wondering about right now. I am trying to understand myself. Sometimes I get to feeling so dry and hollow, like a stuffed animal. Things can get devoid of meaning, feeling can become numbed. I understand that it is I who must keep myself looking straight, but where the hell is the reference point? I can't find my feet. When I am with a girl, I will look into her eyes until I start to shake. I need to see something that will make me understand. At that point, I want to be understood, totally, by her. The rest of the world does not exist, never did I don't see it. I don't know if I ever will. I don't know what I am looking for and it makes me feel dead inside. I sit in a corner after playing, I will go through fits of depression and satisfaction all in a breath. I do not understand what I need to understand and it makes me hurt inside. An understanding of pain is nothing, anyone can stick their hand on a hot plate and go screaming around the house. An understanding of pain is what I want. That's why I look so deep, so hard into their eyes, I look right through. Unfortunately, all I see is myself on the other end, staring right back at me. I feel locked inside for good. Never to breathe, never to understand, never to see outside. All I understand is that everything is starting to run together, their faces, their talk, their touch. Sometimes it feels like being run through a machine. It becomes meaningless, maybe it will come to the point where I will open my eyes and see one of them. I will look into her eyes, hard and see and feel -- nothing.

. . .

Nick, I don't know when or if this will ever get to you but I just thought I'd write anyhow. I am sitting in a most depressing hotel in some Mexican district of S.A. So far on this "jaunt," 46 shows in 46-47 days. I feel a bit worn out. I wrote to you a while ago from Kansas I think, I hope that you got it. I put the letter care of Mute in England, check it out. If this should ever get to you, The Bad Seeds tour will probably be over. I hope it was great and I hope some of it was taped. 34-35 shows still on the schedule. I need a break. We drove all night to get here and I have slept 1-2 hours. I will have to find sleep somewhere. I broke a knuckle on some dude's head in St. Louis, makes writing hard at times. Please make contact with me at some point. If you send a letter, it will be sent to me on the road. I will be in L.A. November 17-19. We are playing at the Palladium, with The Minutemen and The Ramones. The show should be cool. Black Flag tour ends New Year's Eve. January 1-14 I am doing my own tour of reading. I have a lot of people come up and tell me how much they like the Bad Seeds. I think you should try to come here in some capacity at some point. Say hello to anyone I may know.

. . .

Nick, still have this letter, still on tour. 11 weeks now. It is real cold here in Santa Fe, powerful cold. Got a tape of The Bad Seeds show at the Electric Ballroom. The new material is great, no shit. I am doing OK. Show in L.A. sold out, 5,500 people inside, 1,500+ outside rushing doors, a big riot ensued. I have no idea where you are, so I'll just hang onto this until I find out. I hope there will be another Bad Seed recording soon. This cold weather is bullshit. My reading tour is booked. It's real cool, I got some great places to read at. Good and the travel is easy enough. I have been listening to a lot of John Lee Hooker, I made some great tapes of some stuff I bet you have never heard. I got all the stuff from Pettibon, the artist-guy. I hope you are doing OK. I'm sure it's cold as fuck wherever you are. Hang in there. See you at some point, I hope. I'll be in NYC on December 13, and LA by January 14.

. . .

Nick, I mentioned that it was cold in Santa Fe. That was tropical compared to the 35 below zero weather I am in now. You never contact me. I hope you are OK. I am OK. Had to go to the doctor. He said my vocal chords were swollen to three times their normal size, penicillin helped. No shows missed. I need some quiet and some sleep. Be cool.

. . .

9-24-84. Gig ok. Lots of people. Having problems with my throat. Two weeks now, it is starting to annoy and worry me. I very well could be losing my voice. I had my own dressing room, just a room, not much. I found a razor, I starting slamming into my chest. It felt good. I started to bleed, it felt good. There was blood everywhere. The owner came in, saw me, said "excuse me" and bailed. I went into the shower, I turned the water on hard. The water made the cuts in my chest burn. I like the feeling. It's pure and direct and not muddled up by personal, mental, or other trips. I wish everything was a pure, direct, and simple to understand. Just finished sound check. I am having serious throat problems, this is really frustrating. I cannot figure out what it is. It puts me in a really bad mood. I hate throat problems worse than anything, I think. I am gonna have big problems worse than anything. I think. I am gonna have big problems if I can't get it together. I sound like I did two years ago, horse. 9-27-84. In Salt Lake at the Indian center. Pulled in a while ago, all loaded in, now just hanging around. A fellow prison inmate of Manson's lit him on fire with some kind of floor cleaner or something. Burned his face, hands and scalp. I can see him now, sitting in the hospital ward, all wrapped up and shit. I wonder what happens to him now. Will they release him and send him to solitary, or put him back in his normal cell. I feel kind of detached, floating. My writing slacks off in this environment. Oh well. I have thought of things to say and do and write, but often times, they never make it to paper. We are hitting colder weather as we drive eastward. There are two vehicles on this tour. A van and a large Ryder truck. The van carries people and the Ryder carries all the equipment. I live in the Ryder with Davo, Dave and Tom. I like it in there. We take turns being up front and being in back. Being in back is a strange way to travel. You are detached from the drive. I live in total darkness most of the time. I can lie down on a blanket spread over the speakers. The truck makes a lot of noise and it throws you around a lot. You don't know what is happening out there, except for maybe rain on the roof or something. I spend a lot of time in the dark, staring at the ceiling of the truck. I think about a lot of things. I think about this girl, I think about running my hands over her body. I think about her hips. I think about her eyes, I think about her smile. In my mind I come up to her and put my arms out, she pushes me away, not violently but firmly, with determination. She shakes her head slowly "no." Her eyes are fixed to the ground. "No." I turn around without saying a word. I walk away and away and away. I walk forever, through darkness. I look straight ahead, I can see clearly, there is nothing to see. In darkness I can do not wrong. There is a lurching halt. The truck comes to a stop. The door pulls up. Bright Utah sunlight comes streaming in. The darkness vaporizes from my eyes and from my mind. I emerge from the truck. I went into the men's room. I can remember staring at my reflection in the toilet bowl. I can't remember feeling uglier in all my life. 9-28-84. At a diner in Wyoming. Just read the Denver Post's thing on Black Flag. Seems like they like us OK. Morrison thing again. I am getting tired of that shit I tell you. Come on guys, how about some new comparisons like...to Cyndi Lauper, or, hell, I don't know. Last night I met an interesting girl. I was warming up backstage and she started talking to me. She had blond hair down to her waist and bright blue eyes. She was real pretty. She had "Fry Princess" written on her dress. I said "So you are the Fry Princess. I am the Fry Prince." She lunged at me, hair flying all over the place. She said "I knew it, now I feel like dancing!" And she proceeded to jump around and shake her hair around. Then she grabbed me and yelled "I like living here in Salt Lake, you know!" I nodded, more dancing, grabbing, and off the wall comments like "I'm 18, my name is Britt, B-R-I-T-T and I exist just as much as you do!" Now at the

Rainbow in Denver. The Fry Princess said she wanted to come out on stage with me. So when it was time to hit stage, I grabbed her by the hand and took her out there with me, she like it, I introduced her to the audience and said "Fry on, girl!! and she danced off through the side door. What a gal. Pretty nice being back at the Rainbow. I wonder how it will go. I am looking forward to playing. There is starting to be some tension in the ranks. No tension with Rollins, I don't have anybody bothering me. It's snowing outside here in Denver, I don't like snow much, I always figure we will crash the truck or something. It sure was cold in the truck today. Being in the back is like being in a tomb or something, lying prone, wrapped up and waiting for release. I called my mother at her hotel here in Denver. No one home. Maybe she will show, maybe not, it's all the same to me. More on Salt Lake City Utah: we played at the Indian center which is run by Indians. I don't think they were much into us whiteys.

I walked up to the main office where about six of them were seated and asked in there was a backstage area for the band. One said "no," another one, a fat male, said "no, why don't you go change on the street?" There were Indians posted at either side of the stage and in order to get through, you had to show your band stamp. No matter how many times I went by the same guy, he would stop me, grab my hand, scrutinize my hand stamp very carefully, and reluctantly let me pass. I drew a swastika underneath my stamp and went through, that really burned him up, damn! Just having a little fun, no need to get all bent out of shape! In the men's room there was a lot of anti-white-man graffiti on the walls which I thought was real cool. Later on, after the show, an Indian man was sweeping the floor, he walked past me and said, "I should be on that stage, not you!" I just sat there and watched him sweep the floor. Now at Denny's in Denver, show over with now, went OK, challenged all skins to a party but I guess their edges were all straight. About 1/2 the amount of people as last time, but, this is the second time in six months and Rank & File were playing down the street. Played OK. That is the way I always feel about playing on that stage, the show is just "OK." Mom and Les were there tonight.

It was good to see them doing well. Now we go for an overnight drive to Lawrence, Kansas. I feel lonely, the weather and the thought of getting into the truck and freezing does not make me feel all that great. I don't know, I don't like winter-type weather. It snowed today. It was about 29 degrees today. 9-30-84. In a parking lot in Lawrence. It's real nice here, played last night. Good show. Stage a little too high. I wish I had some more time to write but I guess we have to go. The place we stayed reminds me of Dischord House. Omaha, NB -- Just your average hall. I wrote a letter to Nick Cave just now. I don't really feel much like writing right now. I usually don't like to near show time. Slept in some room last night, full of junk and trash. There was a mattress in the middle of it all, got some more sleep in the Rolling Tomb. I was reading from Henry Miller's Tropic of Cancer today while sitting on the ground in Lawrence Kansas. Miller talked about how good everything looks when the sun is out. Even the look in people's eyes. When I was sitting there in Lawrence, the sun was out and everything looked good, perfect, just so. All of a sudden it was the most beautiful place I had ever seen. I could not remember what any other place in the world looked like. I felt like I had been there for a long time. I felt a need to articulate. I could not do it with a photograph, it would have to be with words. Now, hours later, I can only remember the feeling. I can't even remember what Lawrence Kansas looks like. Being here really reminds me of being back in Washington, DC, the people look the same and the streets, houses, and buildings look like Washington. The weather is a contributing factor to this home feeling. I spent a week in Washington in late October '82. Tomorrow is October '84 and I can remember that week now very well and I think the temperature and landscape egg this on. I like to be moving forward so fast that I do not really have a chance to look backwards, it always seems to leave me feeling a bit empty. It's a Sunday night, I'm sitting here in this Bingo Hall in Omaha, Nebraska. It's cold in here. There is no stage, lots of long skinny tables and chairs, the air reeks of that popcorn machine in the front lobby, lots of florescent lights all around. Florescent light makes me feel lonely, crummy.

down. Greg is playing his guitar, 2-3 people who were watching just walked out with their hands over their ears. Later -- Just finished soundcheck. Very loud up there. Later -- Place filling up: I'm sitting at a table, far away from people, lots of people staring at me, pointing and shit. Makes me feel funny. There is no backstage here or I would surely be there. I find more and more that I have less and less to say to people, I just can't get into answering the same questions all the time. This is no fault of theirs. --Twenty minutes later, I just signed about 25-35 autographs, all these people just lined up and started handing me stuff to sign. It makes me feel funny to do that, nice enough people I guess, but still... 10-1-84. Now at the Blue Note in Columbia, Missouri. Pretty easy drive getting here from last night's show. Last night in Omaha was good. I thought we played well. I was grabbing all these girls. It was cool. There was this pretty girl with long hair standing next to her boyfriend I guess, the guy had on a form-fitting rubber mask, looked stupid enough, so I went over and started grinding on the girl,

I don't think either she or her boyfriend liked that much. I grabbed the guy and stuck my tongue through the hole in the mask a ways, the guy really did not like that much at all. I guess there's no pleasing some folks. I like the females from this area. They are genuinely nice girls, at least the ones that come up and talk to me are. They tend to skip the make-up and the fancy clothes. I have nothing to say to any of these girls or anybody else really, most girls get offended when I don't talk to them when they come up to me. I do not like to make idle conversation with people. I feel ugly around girls, I always have, ever since I can remember. I feel like a leper. In darkness I'm not ugly, I'm not anything at all. I like that. I have been with a few girls over the years, not many. I am surprised that I ever got laid in the first place. Stranger things have happened, I guess...They get offended, made. I have heard a lot of things about myself through the mouths of people I have never even met and boy, they sure don't sound too good. This one girl from San Francisco told people that I raped her and beat her up. I sure don't remember doing that but like I said, stranger things have happened. When I walk on the street and I find that I am behind a girl, I always drop back, way back. I don't want the girl to think that I am going to attack her. I have had girls run into stores and wait till I pass before they come out. I just keep my eyes to the ground and try to be low key. This is very hard for me to do. I like the dark. I sit with the lights off a lot if I can. The truck is dark, pitch black, devoid of light, devoid of me. If I can't see my body, then it can't be bad. Today is the first day of October. OK, I like October. Good things happen in October. The leaves turn and all that cool stuff. Last October I was in L.A. That was a drag. That is no place to be if you ask me, I'd rather be somewhere else like Missouri. I hope I don't have to do all that autograph stuff again. Last night was too much. I don't like signing pieces of paper. It makes me feel crummy. I like gigs with dark corners that I can sit in and no one even looks in my general direction. If you don't feel like talking which is pretty much all the time for me, then you have a hard time when someone sits down while you are reading or thinking and starts talking to you. I don't know what to do.

If you say something like "I was reading" or "I'd like to be left alone" that really comes off sounding nasty. I mean that person probably feels embarrassed, stupid and thinks you are conceited when the real deal is that you have been driving all day listening to a lot of talk, loading in equipment, feeling shitty from little sleep, etc. But fuck that! This is no excuse. I guess I am what they say I am. Fine. Turn off the lights and there will be nothing to worry about. In darkness there is nothing but darkness, the sound of my breathing and the absence of light. The eyes. If you can see nothing, then you can see nothing wrong, bad or ugly. I think of that girl when I turn the lights off. She can't see me, but I can see her and she looks real nice tonight... 10-2-84. At the club in Nebraska. Drove all night. After tonight's show, we drive to Minneapolis for two sets. I slept OK last night. I like to sit alone when I eat. I noticed that this seems to offend certain members of the crew. There is just no way that I am going to sit and listen to all that "conversation" when I simply do not have to. Last night's show was OK, I could not hear myself too well so I pushed my voice too hard.

Some guy spat on me and I took his shirt and wiped it off. The fucker...Last night there were these people giving me all these compliments. I don't know what to do. I say "thank you" and try to smile but it comes out funny. I think it's really cool that people dig Black Flag, that's great but I don't know how to handle the compliments. I try to be polite because they are being cool, but I don't take praise well, I never have. I remember when I felt met Nick Cave at the Lingerie Club a couple of years ago. I just held my breath, walked up and introduced myself. He was real cool. I told him he was my favorite singer, (which he still is). That guy looked like he wanted to crawl underneath the table. One time I walked up to Tex Jones from Tex and the Horseheads and told her that I really liked her singing, she smiled like she was really surprised and pleased. When people say they like my singing or something I think that they have brain damage or poor taste. 10-3-84 Pulled into Minneapolis about two hours ago. I have slept about one hour. I feel like I am dead. I took a walk down the street to find coffee. I found a record store and a McDonald's, OK. I went into the record store to look around. I saw Black Flag's new album "Family Man" on the display shelf, not bad. I went into the used record section, I overheard this couple talking as they went through the records: Man: "This place is great! I found the first Black Flag album for three bucks here last week!" Woman: "Three bucks? I'll give you mine for free!" I left the record store and headed into McDonald's. I was feeling like Charles Bukowski inside: 4 lines in front of the counter, mostly male, they looked like they were in line to use the urinal. I was standing behind a woman with a big ass. There was a draft and I caught a breath of what smelled like fresh shit. I thought to myself, "Is this lady shitting her pants? Couldn't she wait until she got to the counter first?" Through the shit stench and urinal queue, was a woman walking in and out of the lines surveying the customers. Asking the kind of questions that those kind of people ask, she looked like a medic during wartime or a stewardess on an airplane. I expect oxygen bags to fall out of the ceiling at any time. I checked out her legs, no shit stains. Got my coffee and crawled through the smoke and the bodies to a fox hole in the front. The phone rang Comfort Woman picked it up: "HELLO! WELCOME TO MCDONALD'S! YES! WELL, PRETTY DARN GOOD! THANK YOU! HAVE A NICE DAY! GOOD BYE!" I made a run for the door, I looked behind me, the McDonald's Courtesy Woman was standing on the counter, she was bleeding from the head, she was yelling into a bullhorn: "Maxine we need some more straws! More Quarter Pounders, Large Fries, Splints, Where's that goddamn plasma! Hit it! Thank you! Pretty darn good! Have a nice day!" I wandered the streets for a time and made it to soundcheck with minor injuries. 10-4-84. Good buddy -- Pulled into Oshkosh about 1-1/2 hours ago. Live in Oshkosh, here is how it went down: pulled into the place, a video-activity-recreation center. Loaded in the P.A. I was running around, humping all this equipment and making lots of Neanderthal sounds, your basic load-in. These girls were staring at me, so I said "Hi, girls. What the...fuck" real D. Boone style, they smiled and walked away. P.A. loaded, I hit the streets in search of COFFEE. I walked down N. Main a few blocks. I saw a "beauty parlour." Inside: women sitting in chairs with huge black cones over their heads, they looked like sub-urban cylons. What was going on in there? Some kind of mid-western brainwashing? Modernized psychotherapy? Plastic surgery while-u-wait? THE ATTACK OF THE BRAIN SUCKERS? Who knows, I didn't stick around long enough to find out. Up ahead in the distance I could see a beacon shining against the evening sky...Burger King. Sure, I had the money -- strong American currency, but would it work here? I ventured in. The man at the counter was so nice just over a cup of coffee it made me cringe. I sat down with my coffee. A man and his son went up to the counter and ordered food. They guy behind the counter smiled at the little boy and said "Hey-y-y! I've got something for you, do you like candy? HERE!" The man handed the kid a red lollipop. I felt like jumping on the counter, pulling out my cock, waving it and screaming "Don't take candy from strangers you little shit!" Busted out of there, walked back down Main and back to Videoland. 10-6-84. In this house that was supposed be "quiet." It's just a bunch of noise.

I don't understand how you can sit around and talk about mundane shit all night long. I'm in this basement, I can hear all these people walking around upstairs, makes a lot of noise. Last night in Oshkosh was real good, cool people, I guess, really into autographs which is a real drag, no dressing rooms so I couldn't hide out. This is nowhere. Tonight's show (10-5-84) was good. I think we played well. I would like to play a little longer really, it seems to go so fast. Rollins out. In Madison. Sitting at a coffee shop. Man, this is some righteous coffee. We are loaded in. I walked here from the hall, not very far really, I kind of know my way around here from previous tours. Outside two lesbians with a cat talk to a man in a wheelchair, a man across from me tells the woman he is sitting with that his friend has A.I.D.S. and it keeps him from sleeping. My father came from this area. I think I can see what happened to him. This is a college town. That's easy to see, I usually do not like college towns much, like Milwaukee and Cleveland, but this place seems to be OK. I guess that we will be here tomorrow since there is no Chicago show. There is probably not much here. I slept in a basement last night. Yesterday when I was walking around Milwaukee, I caught the smell of Katherine Arnold's death again. I wonder what it is. It was just for a second or a minute or so. I was crossing a street and all of a sudden it hit me. All I could think of was that big stain on the retaining wall and the flashlight casting shadows in the grass and that piece of her brain on the wall and that smell...Back at the hall. That coffee shop was a trip. There was this guy behind the counter, he was a gay, and totally wired on coffee. I sat and watched him handle customers. It was great, I thought that he was going to fly through the ceiling. One customer wanted to know the difference between "Nordic Blend," "Viennese Roast," and "Espresso Roast." The request sent this young man into fits. He starting breaking down the coffees like wines. He was great. The store was great. The entire establishment totally devoted to coffee. 10-7-84. At some guy's house in Madison. Last night was good if you ask me. I had a cool time. Slept good. Finished the thing on Katherine Arnold. 10-8-84. Sitting at this guy named Cliff's house.

Cliff is a rich boy. The black van is not here yet, the Ryder came out first. Don't feel all that tired. I'm sitting in a stylish basement. There are Black Flag posters everywhere in the room. I have nothing on my mind so I will stop right here. At this kid's house, talking to the cleaning lady. Decaf on the pot. I drank a cup by mistake. What is this bullshit? 97% caffeine free is 97% not my kind of thing. 10-9-84. At Denny's -- the same Denny's I was at the last time I was in St. Lou. In fact, I am sitting in the same seat even. Last night's show was good. This guy gave me shit so I beat him up pretty bad. I broke his nose something awful. I gave him a lot of chances to back off but he wouldn't so I dealt on him, simple. After the show I had to go way out into the middle of nowhere to do a radio interview -- taped for later use. Went OK. Did not get back until real late. Long drive today. I don't even know where we are playing. I am ready for whatever is coming. I expect nothing but to be led down or to be turned away (Hey man, watch this!) I am alone. Goddamn. The shit hurts sometimes but I realize what I am, what I have become...The alien man waved his arms up and down and noticed that he couldn't wave in the right language so he stopped. In the club. Just got here about 45 minutes ago. Loaded in real fast. Hand all swollen from punching that guy out. I think I broke another knuckle. Walked down to the liquor store to get a soda. Passed a bunch of taxi drivers. They did not like me much judging from the looks on their faces. Walked into the liquor store. The guy in there goes "Good golly gracious, great balls of far!" (sic). Bought a coke. Walked back to the club. A bunch of guys pass me "Alright Henry!" I open the door and walk into the dimly lit hallway, it reeks of sweat and rotting beer. The hunch back owner sits slumped over a stool with a cigarette in his hand. Inside: Ugly woman putting quarters into the jukebox inciting the vomit of John Cougar and Loverboy. It's a Tuesday night, we were here six weeks ago or so. In goes another quarter. Out comes some shit, I don't know who. Pinball game noise, the place stinks of the men's room. Places like this make me sink so low that I think I'm going to melt into the seat I'm in. Loneliness. I am on a lonesome trail.